ATLANTIC PAPER № 64

International Trade in Services: Prospects for Liberalisation in the 1990s

Mario A. Kakabadse

CROOM HELM
London • New York • Sydney
for THE ATLANTIC INSTITUTE FOR INTERNATIONAL AFFAIRS

Croom Helm Ltd, Provident House, Burrell Row,
Beckenham, Kent BR3 1AT

Croom Helm Australia, 44–50 Waterloo Road,
North Ryde, 2113, New South Wales

Published in the USA by
Croom Helm
in association with Methuen, Inc.
29 West 35th Street
New York, NY 10001

British Library Cataloguing in Publication Data

Kakabadse, Mario A.
International trade in services: prospects for liberalisation in the 1990s. — (Atlantic paper; no. 64).
1. Service industries 2. Invisible items of trade
I. Title II. Atlantic Institute for International Affairs
III. Series
382'.453384 HD9980.5

ISBN 0-7099-3130-1

Library of Congress Cataloging in Publication Data

ISBN 0–7099–3130–1

Photosetting by Mayhew Typesetting, Bristol, England
Printed and bound in Great Britain by
Biddles Ltd, Guildford and King's Lynn

Contents

The Author

Dr Mario A. Kakabadse is a Research Associate at the Atlantic Institute for International Affairs. Prior to joining the Institute he was a research consultant with McKinsey & Company and an adviser to the German Government. He has specialised for several years in research and consulting on international marketing and trading issues.

Acknowledgements

The author would like to thank present and former colleagues at the Atlantic Institute for their input and support during the preparation of this study. Thanks are due also to Lee Neumann and Drew Coburn for their research assistance in 1986. Valuable comments were made by John Richardson, Raymond Krommenacker, Knut Hammarskjöld, Marie-Pierre Faudemay and Ken Haydon. The author, of course, is responsible for errors and omissions that remain.

Foreword

Services have long escaped careful study and analysis in the context of international transactions because they are so disparate and because they have usually been considered domestic matters only partially amenable to export. Shipping and air transport have been the traditional pillars of international exchange and as they have been subject neither to the traditional forms of statistical collection nor to the conceptual notions of merchandise trade, they have largely escaped scrutiny and the establishment of viable international rules.

It has become apparent in recent years that manufacturing, the engine of growth in the industrial democracies, has been actually declining in importance, while services, particularly in the information and knowledge areas, have already begun to assume the more significant role. Governments, scholars, and the media are just beginning to come to terms with this phenomenon. Because the extraordinary internationalisation of markets and service suppliers has occurred so quickly, much of current discussion concentrates on matters of articulation and problem identification. In many cases, discussion of solutions to problems must, perforce, lie in abeyance for there is great uncertainty about what problems require solving.

Dr Mario Kakabadse has taken a pioneer step in this study in laying out the broad agenda for international trade in services. His holistic analysis does not pretend to be complete, but he has identified the areas where more comprehensive work needs to be done, where data must be collected, and where government policy makers must place their efforts. Businessmen of all nationalities must applaud this effort, for it is a first cut at bringing coherence to a field where it has long been lacking. The Atlantic Institute's research program will be attempting to fill in some of the gaps which Dr Kakabadse has identified in this study.

Richard D. Vine

Introduction

The service industries and international trade in services have become progressively more important in the economies of both the industrialised and the developing countries. International trade in services has become a critical issue in international economic discussions and will play a central role in the new round of multilateral GATT negotiations. For many countries, some of the most attractive exports are in services offered by such industries as banking, insurance, data processing, telecommunications and tourism.

Major service exporters, such as the United States and France, rely on their large services trade surpluses to offset deficits in merchandise trade but they have increasingly encountered restrictions designed to reduce foreign penetration of domestic markets. There is a vast and diverse array of barriers to trade in services around the world. Recent examples of such protectionism in services include the following:

— to protect the American printing industry, the U.S. Copyright Act prohibits the import of works of American writers printed overseas;
— several countries, including Argentina, Australia and Canada, bar foreign-produced radio and television commercials;
— the transport of agricultural produce from France to the Soviet Union is restricted to vessels of those two countries only;
— an American company using American models for an advertisement in a West German magazine was obliged to hire the models through a German agency, although the advertisement was photographed in the United States;
— an American computer company was prohibited for several years from using private lines to transfer data within Japan as the use

of private lines would have competed with the development of a public data network;
- Japanese airlines get freight cleared more rapidly at Japanese airports than do foreign carriers.

While services have become a substantial and dynamic area of international economic activity, accounting for an estimated one-fifth of total world trade, they have remained outside GATT rules. Except for minor and historically accidental exceptions (notably cinematograph film distribution and exhibition), the GATT did not concern itself with services trade and no significant attempt was made to provide a general framework of international rules for its conduct. It is this gap in the GATT's coverage that has become the focus of attention. This has been due mainly to the initiative of the United States which, since the end of the Tokyo Round, has been urging the inclusion of services in the new round of trade talks. These demands were largely met in the compromise worked out at the Punta del Este conference in September 1986. This major trade conference launched a new round of international trade negotiations known as the Uruguay Round. However, as has been shown by the dispute between the United States, on the one hand, and Brazil and India, the countries most critical of the American approach, on the other, there are formidable conceptual and practical problems still to be overcome before it can be concluded that a global services trade framework is even feasible and politically acceptable, let alone what it should contain.

Part of the problem is rooted in the particular characteristics of international trade in services. Trade in goods and trade in services are different and the rules designed to govern them cannot be the same. Traded goods are shipped across borders but many services, with the exception of those that can be sent along a telephone line, can only be delivered on the spot. Thus, negotiations will have to take into account the fact that protectionism in the area of services means restrictions on foreign investment as much as barriers to trade. New rules for services will have to deal with the question of the right of establishment in the customer's country and will touch upon the sensitive issue of a country's autonomy to make its own foreign investment rules.

An effective conceptual framework for services trade will also have to take into account the rapid technological advances in data processing and telecommunications which are opening up opportunities for significant expansion of international service transactions.

One of the main tasks confronting negotiators will be to avoid the temptation of devising rules appropriate to the current service environment, but not suitable for the environment of the 1990s which is being shaped to a considerable extent by technological innovation. Developing a forward-looking negotiating flexibility towards the international service economy will be no easy task given recent policy responses at the national level. Governments have not been able to keep pace with many technological advances and in several cases have responded with haphazard restrictions and regulatory measures. Given that services everywhere are subject to different degrees of government regulation, services trade negotiations will have to confront contentious issues of national sovereignty and reconcile contradictory views on the legitimate role of government.

Furthermore, the international economic background is not favourable for the launching of the new trade round. Over the past decade, persistent slow growth, rising unemployment, and the commitment of governments to accept responsibility for employment levels and for the survival of particular industries have led to increasing protectionism mainly in the form of domestic or non-tariff border measures. The result of protectionism, subsidies and support for weak industries has been more disputes, weaker rules and further erosion of the multilateral trading system. During the 1980s, protectionist pressures have been intensified by the large and growing imbalances in the world economy, most clearly illustrated by the U.S. deficit and the decline in American competitiveness as a result of the over-valued dollar.

It is clear that the trade talks will take time, and it may well take years, before any kind of multilateral framework for handling services trade can be put in place. The complexity of the issues, the rapid evolution of the service sector and the slow responses of government policies all suggest that domestic and international political consensus — a precondition for the successful negotiation of international commitments — will be difficult to achieve. Indeed, the experience of the Tokyo Round, which lasted from 1973 to 1979, suggests that much work is needed in order to bring about such a consensus before the end of this decade.

This study examines the key issues that the international trading and service communities and governments must address in their attempt to establish a multilateral framework for services trade. Some of the critical questions it addresses are: what are the main driving forces in the major service sectors and how are they affected by barriers to trade? How do technological advances affect the evolution of the service sector and what are the international policy implications? Who are the major players in global service markets and what are their strategies? To what extent are non-OECD countries willing to liberalise their service markets and expose them to the challenge of large U.S., European and Japanese competitors? What are the prospects for agreeing on international rules in services and what concrete progress can be expected over the next five years?

The paper is broken down into four main parts. The first explores the changing role of services in national economies and the changing character of service industries. The second section then analyses the evolving dynamics of the new international service economy and describes some of the important developments in key service sectors. The third lays out the positions of the main participating countries in the negotiations and evaluates the justifications for the existence of governmental restrictions on service transactions. The final part of the study explores how negotiations could be organised to remove existing barriers and to take account of the rapidly changing service environment.

I

The Decline of Manufacturing: The Widening Scope of Services

The service sector has been increasing its share of both output and employment in the industrialised countries. The general shift towards a more service-oriented economy represents a change of historic significance. It has been determined by a number of factors, including the increased demand for consumer services and leisure goods, the growing need by business for services — marketing, accounting and others — traditionally provided internally by the manufacturing firm, and the greater demand by government, a major consumer of goods and services. In addition, technological advances, in particular in the area of information technology, are rapidly improving methods of production, management and delivery of services.

The Question of Definition

Despite their notable rise in both economic importance and analytical interest, services have eluded satisfactory definition, in part because they range over a wide number of activities.[1] The conventional approach uses the traditional division of national economies into primary, secondary and tertiary sectors to define services as the residual economic activity not included under agriculture, mining and manufacturing. One of the problems with this traditional classification is that it tends to overlook the fact that service functions are performed in various sectors of the economy. On a more theoretical level, other definitions focus on the intangible, non-transportable and non-storable qualities commonly associated with service 'products', thus giving rise to the pragmatist's view that 'services are something you can buy and sell

Table 1: Classification of Services and Key Technological Developments

Sector	Key technological developments
Construction service: — construction and engineering (project planning, execution and management, consulting, training)	— new techniques in communications, control and measurement, CAD/CAM for design, construction, installation and transport — new construction techniques using large-scale units in modern materials — new surface and protective coatings using resins
Distributive services: — goods transport (air, road, rail, waterways) and storage — travel (passenger transport) — shipping — retail trade — wholesale trade	— automated rail terminals and traffic control systems, standardised train composition — improved engine performance via microprocessor/sensor analysis — computerised warehouse procedures to increase efficiency: planning and ordering systems, automatic pallet loading/unloading, book-keeping — large scale door-to-door service for containers facilitated by improved information/communications systems — automated reservation and ticket systems — automated stock control linked to cash-register systems (bar code, optical scanners at check-outs) — point-of-sale equipment for cheque validity tests — growth of mail-order via teleshopping — computerised warehouse procedures
Financial and Insurance services: — banking and other financial services — insurance and reinsurance — brokerage (transport and insurance) — trusts and building societies	— introduction of data processing in and between companies for banks — automated book-keeping and processing of payments — cash dispensers and automated teller machines — automated credit saving — credit card payment systems — computerisation of insurance — use of value added networks (VANs) for cheap and effective communication

Commercial services: — professional and business support services (incl. accounting, advertising, design, technical and management consulting, legal services, computer services, translation, copying and temporary employment, architectural services, leasing, franchising, trade fairs) — auto-rental agencies — real estate — repairs and maintenance, cleaning services — news and press agencies — motion pictures, printing and art work	— increased employee access to internal/external data bases via introduction of information processing, office automation — IT for decision support systems, financial modelling, information retrieval systems — growth of software development in computer service companies — new security techniques: remote-controlled TV, monitoring systems, remote-controlled access and exits, etc.
Telecommunications and information services: — telecommunications (telephone, telegraph, television, teledata transmission) — data processing (computer treatment of information base)	— merging of separate networks for telex, telephony and data traffic into single communications network is key to development of office automation affecting in particular financial and professional services — development of satellite communications: multinational service companies (banks, insurance companies, media companies, hotel chains) will acquire own satellite data transmission networks

Table 1: Continued

Sector	Key technological developments
Collective services: — health care — education and research — social welfare services — government services	— data computerisation, office automation, more efficient catering, electronic diagnostic techniques, monitoring equipment, new pharmaceutical products — telecommunications for in-service training — growth of computer/software suppliers competing with traditional textbook publishers — automation of advisory services and administration
Personal services: — hotel and catering services — tourism (tour operating) — leisure, recreational and cultural services — domestic services and personal care (hairdressing, dry-cleaning, etc.)	— cost efficiencies via leasing/acquiring satellite for hotel chains and conference centres — automation of reservations and booking systems particularly by travel agencies — increase in number of local radio and TV networks and international links — application of CAD techniques for various types of design

but cannot drop on your foot'. However, this is by no means an all-encompassing definition as numerous services actually do produce physical outputs, such as written reports, computer discs, magnetic tapes and film. In these cases the relevant information storage media may be considered as goods which can be transported and stored and which at the same time are the technical means with which the actual service — the provision of information — can be performed.

In the absence of commonly accepted operative definitions, the next-best approach to characterising the service industry has led to a direct classification and categorisation of the various activities and professions encompassed. Although providing considerable clarity and precision, the substitution of lists of services for definitions of services has at least two potential drawbacks. First, the list must remain open-ended as marketing and technological innovations are continually creating new services. Second, such lists clearly contain a degree of subjectivity with differing views of what constitutes particular service sectors. To be suitable as a starting point for further thinking, a classification system should combine both an institutional or functional approach and some indication of the kind of change that different sectors are undergoing. Table 1 attempts to summarise the prime service industry categories in relation to the key technological developments that are affecting their future shape. The list, far from pretending to be complete, merely points the way to further research issues which are relevant to government and business policy makers.[2] It demonstrates the type of dynamic classification which must be used for future analysis and as a basis for negotiations.

Services in the Domestic Economy

A summary of the size and growth of major sectors in the five leading OECD economies in terms of employment and output is presented in Tables 2 and 3. In the United States and Japan non-governmental or market services (here taken to include construction) account for well over half of GDP, and in the United Kingdom, France and West Germany the proportion is between 40 and 50 percent. In terms of employment the picture is similar, with the market service sector accounting for 59 percent of total employment in the United States in 1983. If workers in government services are added, over three-quarters of the U.S. working population are classifiable as service workers. In the United Kingdom and France

Table 2: The Relative Size and Growth of Major Sectors in the Leading Industrial Economies: GDP

	USA		France		FRG		Japan		UK[a]
	Share of GDP 1983 (in %)	Av. annual growth 1970–83 (in %)	Share of GDP 1983 (in %)	Av. annual growth 1970–83 (in %)	Share of GDP 1982 (in %)	Av. annual growth 1970–82 (in %)	Share of GDP 1983 (in %)	Av. annual growth 1970–83 (in %)	Share of GDP 1983 (in %)
Primary	5	0.8	5	0.5	4	1.8	4	0.5	9
Manufacturing[b]	24	2.3	28	3.1	35	3.3	34	7.0	24
Services									
— Market[c]	58	3.2	49	3.5	47	4.9	56	4.5	43
— Government	13	1.2	13	2.3	12	4.7	9	3.8	14
Total[d]	100	2.6	95	3.8	98	4.0	103	4.8	90
Absolute GDP	$ 3280 billion		FF 3935 billion		DM 1600 billion		Y 2750 hundred billion		£ 300 billion

a. Figures not available for average annual growth
b. Includes utilities
c. Includes construction
d. Taxes, duties, and other adjustments included in GDP cause apparent discrepancies for UK, France, FRG and Japan
Source: OECD, *National Accounts*

Table 3: The Relative Size and Growth of Major Sectors in the Leading Industrial Economies: Employment

	USA		France		FRG		Japan		UK[a]
	Empl't 1983 (in %)	Av. annual growth 1970–83 (in %)	Empl't 1983 (in %)	Av. annual growth 1975–83 (in %)	Empl't 1982 (in %)	Av. annual growth 1970–82 (in %)	Empl't 1983 (in %)	Av. annual growth 1970–83 (in %)	Empl't 1981 (in %)
Primary	4	0.5	8	−1.9	6	−4.7	12	−3.0	2
Manufacturing[b]	18	−0.3	24	−0.3	34	−1.8	25	1.7	29
Services									
— Market[c]	59	2.6	48	2.6	41	0.4	55	2.4	47
— Government	18	0.9	19	0.9	16	2.2	7	1.7	22
Total (absolute)	108 million	1.6	22 million	1.6	26 million	−0.4	62 million	0.9	24 million

a. Figures not available for average annual growth
b. Includes utilities
c. Includes construction
Source: OECD, *National Accounts*

the figures are 69 and 67 percent respectively. In all the developed countries 'knowledge' or 'information' workers represent the largest section of the labour force and even in manufacturing, knowledge or information workers will probably outnumber blue-collar workers by the end of the century.

The character of the manufacturing sector is evolving and two distinct kinds of industry are emerging. One is the traditional, raw material-based, producing sector which was the engine of economic growth during the nineteenth century and the first seven decades of this century. The other is knowledge and information-based, comprising such industries as electronics, telecommunications equipment, analytical instruments, pharmaceuticals and computers. Generally, it is the information-based manufacturing industries that are growing. According to the U.S. Commerce Department's annual survey of American industry, economic growth continues to be led by such high technology industries as semiconductors, computers, optical devices, telephone equipment and X-ray apparatus.[3] It should be noted that the workforce requirements of this second category are quantitatively smaller and qualitatively much more demanding than for the traditional sector of the manufacturing industry.

The same report also states that in addition to high technology industries services will continue to be the other engine of GNP growth. Ranked according to estimated growth, the top ten service industries are: mutual funds (assets), legal services and management consulting (calculated for both in terms of receipts), life insurance (premium receipts), health and medical services, savings institutions (deposits), motor vehicle dealers, hotels and motels, commercial banking (deposits) and franchising (franchisors' sales).

Most of the new knowledge-based jobs are in service industries which are in the business of creating, processing and selling information. As the Commerce Department findings show, many of these industries are among the fastest growing in the U.S. economy. Information is compiled by a growing number of data-base companies which provide direct access to computer-based information on anything from health care data to airline schedules. Professional service companies in management consulting, engineering, law and accounting sell specialised information. Other kinds of information are provided by publishers, record and videotape companies, and even film studios. Computer-service suppliers, printers and key-punching companies are involved in data processing, while information distribution is provided by telephone companies, specialist communication companies and bookshops.

As Table 3 shows, growth in employment in the market services sector has been faster than in any other sector in the American, French and Japanese economies. This increase of domestic employment, and the growing realisation that the exporting of knowledge to generate royalties, license income and service fees may in time create more jobs than exporting goods. These developments require that much more emphasis be placed in trade policy on 'invisible trade' and on reducing barriers to services trade. In the major developed countries, where services account for high and increasing proportions of employment and output, freer trade in services will soon be vital. Traditionally, invisible trade has been neglected by economic analysis but it is becoming increasingly central as the governments of the OECD countries become aware of the importance of income from invisible trade and conscious of the need to measure it accurately.

As in the industrialised countries of Europe and North America, the role of the service sector in Japan has expanded rapidly in the past fifteen years and will continue to grow in importance in the future. By 1983, the market services sector accounted for 55 percent of total employment, and the Japanese government has projected that this figure will rise to nearly 62 percent by the end of the century.[4] In GDP terms, the service industry generated 56 percent of total production, a figure that is expected to grow by eight percentage points by the year 2000. Present levels of employment and GDP contribution by Japan's service sector are comparable to those in the United States and are considerably greater than those in the major industrialised countries of Europe. In all the advanced economies, as can be seen from Tables 4 and 5, retailing plays a central role, accounting for about one-third of total service sector employment and roughly one-quarter of overall output.

There are, however, large differences in productivity: the OECD reckons that Japanese productivity in the retail and wholesale trade — where cartels play an important role in distribution and where small shops are legally protected against competition from supermarkets and chainstores — is equal to only half of that in the United States.[5] In banking and finance, regulatory protection is being reduced partly in response to foreign pressure on Japan to expand the international use of the yen. The volume of foreign financial institutions moving to Tokyo indicates that Japan's financial markets have developed a degree of international compatibility exceeding the most optimistic expectations of five years ago.

Table 4: The Market Services Sector: Comparative Structure and Growth of Employment in 1983

	USA Empl't (m)	USA % share	USA grow rate (a)	UK Empl't (m)	UK % share	UK grow rate (b)	France Empl't (m)	France % share	France grow rate (a)	FRG Empl't (m)	FRG % share	FRG grow rate (c)	Japan Empl't (m)	Japan % share	Japan grow rate (a)
Construction	5.3	8	1.4	1.4	12	−0.2	1.7	16	−1.4	1.9	18	−2.1	5.9	18	1.9
Wholesale/retail	23.2	36	2.4				2.9	28	0.8	3.4	33	−0.1	10.9	32	1.7
Restaurant/hotels	1.6	3	3.2				0.64	6	1.4						
Transport/storage	3.1	5	0.6	1.5	13	−0.2	0.89	8	0.5	1.0	10	−0.3	3.5	10	1.0
Communications	1.4	2	2.0				0.48	5	2.2	0.51	5	0.7			
Finance	2.8	4	4.2				0.45	4	1.9	0.55	5	2.0			
Insurance	1.9	3	2.6				0.22	2	2.0	0.20	2	0.5			
Business services (incl. real estate)	8.0	13	5.7				0.93	9	3.9				2.5	8	2.8
Real estate/ dwellings				8.5	75	1.5									
Personal services	16.7	26	2.7				2.3	22	3.6	2.9	28	1.8	10.9	32	3.5
— health	6.4	10	5.4												
— personal & household	4.7	7	0.2				0.52	5	0.9						
— recreational	1.2	2	3.7				0.14	1	−2.7						
— educational	1.5	2	1.9												
— other	2.9	5													
Total	64.0	100	2.6	11.4	100	n.a.	10.5	100	2.6	10.4	100	0.4	33.7	100	2.4

Note: Growth rate refers to average annual compound growth (%); (a) 1971–83; (b) 1971–81; (c) 1971–82
Source: OECD, *National Accounts*

Table 5: The Market Services Sector: Comparative Structure and Growth (GDP Volume)

	USA			UK			France			FRG			Japan		
	$ bn.	% Serv. sect.	% ann. grow	£ bn.	% Serv. sect.	% ann. grow	FF bn.	% Serv. sect.	% ann. grow	DM bn.	% Serv. sect.	% ann. grow	100 Y bn.	% Serv. sect.	% ann. grow
Construction	133	7	−1.4	15.3	12	−2.1	236	12	−0.4	96.4	13	−0.3	217	14	1.6
Wholesale/retail	533	28	3.1	35.0	27	−0.2	387	20	2.8	153	21	1.7	335	22	4.8
Restaurants/hotels	24	1	2.6				88	5	0.7	20.5	3	0.9			
Transport/storage	116	6	0.9	18.6	14	0.9	150	8	−1.2	56.7	8	2.1	191	12	3.8
Communications	93	5	6.6				56	3	8.3	36.8	5	6.8			
Finance	100	5	3.5							71.7	10	5.3			
Insurance	56	3	2.5							16.9	2	3.9			
Business services (inc. real estate)	273	14	4.7	46.8	36	3.8	684	35	4.4	93.7	13	3.5	464	30	6.7
Real estate/ dwellings	303	16	4.3												
Personal services	285	15	3.3	14.0	11	3.2	331	17	5.2	190	26	4.5	341	22	3.2
— health	152	8	4.9							35.8	4	4.1			
— personal & household	56	3	0.5												
— recreational	25	1	4.9							154	22	4.6			
— educational	20	1	1.8												
— other	32	2													
Total	1916	100	3.2	129.7	100	n.a.	1932	100	2.6	735	100	4.9	1550	100	4.5

Note: Growth rate refers to average annual compound growth: UK 1979–83; USA, France and Japan 1970–83; FRG 1970–82.
Source: OECD, *National Accounts*.

Transformation of Services

A major problem in evaluating the role of services in domestic economies is the blurring of the distinction between goods-producing and service-producing industries. Some of the rapidly growing services, such as data processing, engineering design, and construction abroad are often linked to transactions in goods, the two forming a package. In trading terms, for example, the export of computers is usually accompanied by the sale of computer software and engineering design, or foreign construction is tied to the sale of machinery and equipment.

In addition, in North America, Europe and Japan manufacturing companies have been undergoing a process of reorganisation, not only in response to changing economic conditions but also to technological innovation. This has involved a double-sided process.

First, there has been the steadily increasing practice of shifting service functions from employees within companies to outside service firms. Evidence from the United States, in particular, suggests that the category of business services has been among the most expansive. Table 4 shows that in the United States there are 8 million people employed in the business services sector (which for lack of a more detailed statistical breakdown also includes real estate brokerage). In terms of rate of increase of employment this has been the fastest growing sector with an average annual rate of 5.7 percent growth and has been a major factor contributing to the recent recovery of employment in the United States.

Leading services in this area are personnel supply, computers and data processing, advertising, stenographic services and services to buildings. According to the U.S. Department of Labor, by 1995 more than 2.6 million new business sector jobs are projected to be added to 1984's level of 4.6 million — an annual growth rate of 4.2 percent. Growth in business services can be attributed to a combination of factors, the most important being that many new kinds of services have become integral parts of current business operations — technological advances have led to an increased demand for programming and software services and for a whole range of consulting and management services. Firms have found it more efficient to contract out many of these services to specialists who can enjoy economies of scale.

Similar to the United States, the United Kingdom has recorded its highest employment growth rates in the sector of financial, business, professional and scientific services with the total number employed rising from 4.3 million in 1973 to nearly 5 million by 1983.[6] To the extent that firms replace their workers with outside specialists, a shift in employment from manufacturing to services occurs. In such cases there is no basic change in the type of work being done, but there is a major change in how and where the work is performed, resulting in a different industrial classification.

Second, manufacturing companies have at the same time been incorporating new information-based services into their own structures and diversifying the services provided to customers. Consequently, they have also widened the geographical range of their operations. One of the most remarkable examples of this process has been the restructuring of General Electric (GE) by grouping its fifteen 'critical' businesses into three categories: core manufacturing, high technology and services. As a result of comprehensive restructuring, GE's traditional orientation as a consumer and industrial electrical products manufacturer is rapidly changing. This is reflected in the shift in the composition of its earnings: in 1980 core manufacturing was the mainstay of the company, contributing 46 percent of total earnings, with high technology and services accounting for 31 percent and 23 percent respectively. Five years later, manufacturing's share had declined to 22 percent of total earnings while the contributions from the high technology and service sectors had risen to 40 and 38 percent respectively. The fact that services are the fastest growing part of GE's business is indicative of the company's goal of becoming a major participant in the financial services market and reflects the growing interest of large corporations in acquiring high-growth service-oriented companies in areas outside their traditional manufacturing sphere.[7]

The shape of service industries is also being transformed by mergers and acquisitions which help to blur traditional service boundaries. Banks become travel agents, textile retailers become credit card companies, securities houses apply for banking licences, insurance agents sell investment advice, and transport companies attempt to optimise their existing infrastructure by offering additional services through their existing outlets and systems. In particular, the American banking landscape (in which the activities of American banks are highly circumscribed) provides an outstanding example of the blurring of traditional service boundaries. Among the several non-bank giants competing for a share of the consumer banking market are Detroit's captive finance houses — Ford Credit, Chrysler Financial and General Motors Acceptance Corporation — which have been acquiring financial service companies to add to their core business of financing dealer sales. Sears Roebuck, the largest retailer in the United States with a network of 800 stores and 60 million credit card customers, not only extends credit but accepts deposits and is aiming to provide consumer financial services electronically. Like other large insurers, Prudential is offering, through its brokerage firm Prudential-Bache, certificates of deposit, mortgages, mutual funds and retirement accounts.

The Impact of Technology

Much of the changing character of service industries is coming about through the development and application of a range of new technologies which are increasing the productivity of certain service industries as fast as, if not faster than, factory automation or robotics are doing in manufacturing. The creation, processing and transmission of information have become a key growth sector in the international economy, and, particularly when supported by moves towards national deregulation in some service industries, are having a significant impact on international competition and trade. Developments in microelectronics and applications in computerisation and telecommunications have widened the range of services that can be made available. Moreover, the declining cost of microelectronic products has made the use of data banks and advanced communication services more accessible to a wider range of competitors of all sizes. Many new kinds of services are being made available, from the provision of software for the management and delivery of engineering services to the supply of highly sophisticated retailer support systems.

The entire retailing industry is going through a remarkable process of transformation made possible by the convergence of computing and communications. Companies that have appreciated this technological potential have been able to develop significant competitive advantages. In the grocery trade the development of bar codes and scanning, either built into the check-out counter or in light-pen form, is the most significant innovation since the advent of the supermarket. In the United Kingdom, the commitment of major chainstores such as Sainsbury, Tesco and Asda to scanning makes it likely that the bulk of British supermarkets will have scanning check-outs by the end of the decade. These groups, and their counterparts in Europe and the United States, are not only impressed by the speed and accuracy of such technology but also by the so-called 'soft' benefits from the investment in electronic technology — improvements in management information and control of merchandise as it moves through the business. It is in this area that the greatest potential productivity increases and savings are to be found.

Point-of-sale terminals in shops, bar-coding on products and the increasing use of credit cards have made it simpler for businesses to pinpoint their customers and their buying habits. Another recent development is in the field of electronic funds transfer at the point of sale (EFTPOS), a system whereby a customer has his account debited directly at the check-out by using a special charge card and terminal. For the retailer and banker this method promises faster and more efficient transfer of funds which should help to keep costs down. The growing interest of retailers in technology is seen also in computer shopping which is being undertaken on an experimental basis in a few countries. The system, which is now in its infancy but likely to grow quite rapidly in the next few years, offers the customer advantages similar to those offered by mail order with the added convenience that it can give access to a wider range of stores and that the computerised catalogues are fully up to date.

Technology has also redefined the role of grocery wholesaling, once thought to have been made obsolete by the development of large supermarket chains. In the United States, the highly successful grocery wholesale operation called Super Valu — where only fifteen executives at its Minneapolis headquarters run a 15 billion dollars business — claims 'to be able to make an independently owned supermarket as efficient and productive as a chain competitor of equal size, primarily through the use of several computer-oriented analytic devices.'[8]

There are several information-related sectors that make direct use of developments in the communications and electronics industries. Significant information-related services — those in which the majority of activities relate to information processing and transmission — include suppliers of seminal value-added services in the financial sector: banks, credit card companies, bond dealers, capital and stock exchanges,[9] currency, commodities and futures markets, the insurance industry and estate agents. Electronic forms of information storage and transmission are increasingly important to service businesses that rely on complex reservation systems, such as airlines, travel agents, hotel chains and car rental companies. 'Hertz and other leading auto rental agencies,' notes Professor James Heskett, 'have implemented sophisticated inventory control programs based on more timely data from their thousands of rental desks. Hertz thereby positions its inventory more effectively, obtains greater utilization per vehicle, and reduces the need for some inventory. Hertz and its competitors are substituting information for assets.'[10]

Large investments in new technology are an essential characteristic of the banks. According to Salomon Brothers, the New York securities firm, the leading American banks spent 7 billion dollars on electronic banking technology between 1980 and 1985 and devoted 11–15 percent of their non-interest expenditure to automation. This proportion is higher than in any other industry except the data-processing industry itself. The current expenditure figure of French banks on *informatique* is also of the order of 15 percent, surpassing for the first time the amount spent on premises.[11]

The exploitation of electronic technology by the world's major financial institutions can be roughly divided into three phases. In the first phase, driven mainly by technologists, banks introduced automation to reduce their internal operating costs and set up a cheap and reliable payments mechanism by computerising the accounting and clearing functions in the 'back office'. In the second phase, which took off in the mid-1970s, bankers began to think about exploiting the potential of computer-based systems to support new products and services to extend their customer base. Several new developments date back to this era: electronic funds transfer at the point-of-sale, cashless shopping, automated teller machines (ATMs) and projects for substantial networks of ATMs. At the international level, the Society for Worldwide Interbank Financial Telecommunication (SWIFT) is an electronic message service working for more than 1,400 member banks. SWIFT has become a unifying force in global banking, forcing banks to standardise their banking procedures so that each bank uses the same format for similar services. At the current time, banks are entering a third and new phase which is characterised by deeper reflection on the commercial and financial implications of installing new technology. International banking information networks are maturing in terms of size, sophistication and power but there is also growing concern about the security and integrity of the masses of data moving around the world at high speed. Banks, trusts and building societies, which have all built up huge amounts of computerised data, are now looking more closely at the problem of how to use that information more efficiently for commercial advantage. Many in the industry feel that a great deal of work is necessary to convert the often haphazardly accumulated customer data bases into truly integrated customer files to exploit marketing opportunities better.

Like banking, the insurance business lends itself well to computerisation. Computer systems are particularly suited to the key tasks of performing complex calculations and handling large amounts of historical data and carefully worded documentation. Extensive use is being made of value added networks (VANs) which offer insurers the most efficient way of communicating with each other. Insurers are trying to find agreement on standard, industry-wide message formats on the SWIFT model. Geisco, a large American computer services company and VANs operator, is marketing its idea to brokers and insurers of a global electronic register of information about clients and their contracts that would replace much of the paperwork which still takes up so much time in the industry.

Deregulation

Technological change has also encouraged the trend towards deregulation in certain sectors (most widely practised in the United States in recent years) because it has increased the ability of companies of all sizes to compete with each other, often through the use and adaptation of new technologies. The regulatory protection traditionally afforded to both service suppliers and customers has increasingly become an obstacle to technological change. Deregulation has accelerated the transformation of service industries.

The deregulation of almost the entire transportation sector in the United States has shown how competitive forces can assert themselves to improve efficiency and cut costs. In some cases, the main results have been to bring prices into line with costs of services, and in others, competition has been introduced by removal of regulatory restrictions. In the process several companies have gone bankrupt (more than 300 in the U.S. trucking industry alone), but many more have been created, including more than 10,000 small new trucking companies. On the basis of this experience, it seems reasonable to assume that deregulation itself will speed the process of technological innovation and its application in service industries.

In the areas of finance and communication, the consequences of U.S. domestic deregulation are already significant for other countries. The strong increase in trading of financial instruments of all kinds and the intensified speed with which relevant information is available for decision making are helping force governments to deregulate their domestic money and capital markets. In telecommunications, the pace of technological change — driven by the convergence of data processing with communications technology — is forcing many governments to reevaluate their role in this field: following the American example, the governments of Japan, Canada and the United Kingdom are liberalising, to varying degrees, their telecommunications service industries.

Concluding Observations

This brief review of significant domestic developments in the service sectors of the advanced industrial economies highlights a few outstanding characteristics. First, the increased dependence on services of the major industrialised economies in the last fifteen years has been remarkable. What may be termed a process of deindustrialisation has occurred in the sense that services now account for a larger proportion of economic activity. This has been more marked in employment than in output terms. According to traditional measures, the service sector in each accounts for the major part of economic activity, and indeed the growth in demand for services is in large measure a reflection of primary and secondary sector demand.

Second, measured in terms of rate of growth of output, productivity gains in the service sector in the United States, France and Germany have been higher than corresponding gains in manufacturing, contradicting the view of conventional theory which stresses the inherently low productivity of the service sector. In this respect, a closer look at productivity advances in the German service sector could indicate that German efforts to innovate or apply new technologies to service sector activities have been more successful than in other major countries during recent years. In Japan, productivity gains in the service sector have been lower than gains in manufacturing, one reason being that until recently productivity increases realised through the application of technology have occurred primarily in manufacturing. This may be due partly to the fact that Japanese entrepreneurs seek out profitable service substitutes with more zest than their Western counterparts. Opportunities for tangible goods to replace or substitute personalised services exist both at the productive level (computers replacing clerks) and at the level of the final service needs of consumers (labour-saving devices in the home, provision of entertainment via video and other electronic means).

Third, except in Germany, the growth of the services' share in GDP has been accompanied by substantial increases also in their share of employment and, presumably, wages. The recent recovery of employment in the United States has been almost entirely due to the growth of the service sector.

Fourth, these findings, and a growing number of studies being carried out around the world, are leading to a revision of conventional theory which views the growth of services as the result of a development process consisting of three main phases: the pre-industrial phase, the industrial phase and the post-industrial phase, in which the economy shifts from manufacturing to services. Intangible investment in data service systems is becoming a more important resource than investment in plant and machinery in all areas of the economy. In Japan, for example, much rethinking about the shift from 'hard' to 'soft' technologies and the growing role of invisible service functions is going on under the label of 'softnomics', which emphasises their knowledge-intensive aspects.[12]

It is important to recognise that the significance of services goes beyond what can be expressed in terms of traditional measures of productivity. Given the incorporation of a continuously growing number of services in the industrial sector, economic efficiency depends to an increasing extent on the interlinkages between the different productive activities and not only on the productive conditions in the activities themselves. Thus, an efficient and well-managed banking system, transportation network, insurance industry, telecommunications sector and public administration are all vital for growth and development.

II

The New International Service Economy

Although the role of services within the national setting has been mushrooming, the narrower set of internationally traded services only amounts to about 8 percent of the world's production of services. What are the dynamics of the new international service economy? In attempting to address this question, this chapter examines two key problems. First, it identifies the main trends in the international service economy, taking into account the major weaknesses of the international comparative data base — that of the International Monetary Fund (IMF) — that is currently most generally used. Second, it examines the most important factors shaping competition in international service markets and how they differ between sectors.

To an important degree, international trade in services tends to differ from international trade in goods in terms of the linkages between the producer and the consumer or user of the product. All goods are tradeable in the sense that they can be produced in one country and sold in another, either by transporting them across a border or by marketing them through the manufacturer's local affiliate. This does not apply to all services. There are some services, of course, such as data bases or software that can be sold abroad via the international telecommunications network and although this type of trade is expanding it does not generally apply to other services. For a whole range of services — such as many traditional education and health services, hairdressing, retailing, catering, and inland passenger transport — the supplier and consumer are required to be present in the same place at the same time. In most of these cases, the services produced in one country are not sold to consumers in another country, thus rendering a very large part of a country's service output non-tradeable.

Table 6: World Trade in Goods and Services (at current value in U.S. $ billions)

	1970	1975	1980	1983	Compound Annual Growth (1970–83) %
TOTAL	375.4	1023.5	2398.5	2034.9	13.9
Merchandise	282.6	798.2	1855.7	1508.4	13.7
Invisibles	92.8	225.3	542.3	526.5	14.3
— transport	25.9	59.5	129.4	114.5	12.1
— foreign travel	20.7	42.3	99.0	89.0	11.9
— investment	26.6	69.5	189.5	194.0	16.5
— other	19.6	54.0	124.8	129.0	15.6
Invisibles/world trade (%)	24.7	22.0	22.6	25.9	
Services[a]/world trade (%)	17.6	15.2	14.7	16.3	

a. Invisibles less investment income
Source: IMF, *Balance of Payments Statistics*

In many traded services the same principle applies: either the consumer has to be physically transported to the product (tourism) or the service has to be taken to the consumer, usually by means of an established presence of the supplier in the importing country. Although this latter factor also occurs in goods trade through foreign direct investment, where marketing and management know-how are significant aspects of the product, an established presence is particularly important in the case of services. In banking, for example, most services can only be supplied by some form of foreign direct investment to establish a local presence in the form of a branch, agency or subsidiary. In this sense, the activities of a foreign commercial presence can be considered part of a working definition of international trade in services.

Global Trends in Services Trade

Some idea of the size of world trade in services and the identity of the main suppliers and markets can be derived from IMF balance-of-payments statistics. The IMF estimates that in 1983 the value of trade in so-called invisibles represented about 26 percent of total world trade. As can be seen from Table 6 the largest single category is investment income which is derived from direct investment in foreign subsidiaries and associates, and through the money and capital markets. When this category is excluded, trade in services — comprising transport, travel and other services — amounted to nearly 333 billion dollars or 16 percent of world trade. Travel and transportation include all expenditures connected with the international movement of people, and the goods and services bought by travellers outside their country of residence. 'Other services' is a crucial category representing receipts and payments on private services such as construction, insurance and finance.

Given the widespread impression that services trade has been growing at a strong pace, it is perhaps surprising to note that, in global terms, between 1970 and 1983 the average annual compound growth rate for the travel and transport sectors (each around 12 percent) lagged behind the rate of growth of merchandise exports (13.7 percent). The only service category which grew faster than trade in goods was 'other services' which includes many of the newer and more dynamic service sectors. It is important to note, however, that between 1980 and 1983, while merchandise trade declined in value terms by a margin of 19 percent, trade in invisibles

Table 7: Breakdown of Service Receipts by Country (1983)

Rank	Country	Total invisible receipts[a] (bn $)	Total service receipts (bn $)	Service receipt as % of total trade receipts	Breakdown of services receipts		
					Transp. %	Travel %	Other %
1.	USA	111.6	39.4	13	40	29	31
2.	France	53.8	35.5	25	26	20	54
3.	UK	44.5	26.5	19	32	21	47
4.	FRG	36.2	27.7	14	29	20	51
5.	Japan	30.9	19.8	11	62	4	24
6.	Bel./Lux.	29.6	11.8	16	28	14	58
7.	Italy	25.2	21.0	22	21	43	36
8.	Netherlands	22.2	13.5	16	57	10	33
9.	Switzerland	17.3	7.8	18	17	41	42
10.	Austria	12.0	9.4	34	7	56	36
11.	Spain	11.9	11.4	35	25	60	15
12.	Canada	11.6	7.5	9	16	41	43
13.	Singapore	9.0	8.0	31	32	22	46
14.	Sweden	8.0	6.8	19	40	16	44
15.	Norway	8.0	7.3	28	68	9	23
TOTAL WORLD (bn $)		526.5	332.5		114.5	89.0	129.0
Share of top five		53%	45%		47%	45%	50%
Share of top ten		73%	64%		68%	68%	72%

a. Service receipts plus foreign investment income
Source: IMF, *Balance of Payments*

remained more or less constant. World production has been growing more slowly than trade in any of these sectors and so one can conclude that international trade in services is steadily expanding its share of world output at a similar pace to that of goods.

The industrialised countries are both the largest producers and consumers of traded services. The United States, the leading exporter of services, sold services abroad of 39.4 billion dollars in 1983, about 12 percent of the world total. In the case of the United States the large discrepancy between total invisible receipts (112 billion dollars) and total service receipts is evident; when investment income is excluded the United States no longer holds a dominant position among the major international suppliers of services. The IMF data, summarised in Table 7, shows the United States, France, the United Kingdom, West Germany and Italy to be the world's leading exporters of services, accounting between them for nearly half of the world total. The top fifteen service exporting countries accounted for over three-quarters of total global service exports in 1983 and among them only one, Singapore, was a developing country.

The figures also give a breakdown of service exports by type of service. Thus, the crucial 'other' service category plays a dominant role in the services trade of France, the United Kingdom, West Germany, Belgium, Switzerland, Sweden and Singapore. Surprisingly, in the case of both Japan and the United States this sector accounts for less than one-third of total services trade revenues. These figures are the only ones which permit international comparison, but recent research has indicated that this data on the volume and value of traded services most likely understates by a considerable margin the share of services in total trade activity. By 1983, world trade in services (excluding investment income) reported by governments had reached 333 billion dollars but because data on international service transactions are seriously incomplete, the real figure is probably much higher. No one has yet worked out how much greater the figure could be at the global level, although the U.S. Office of Technology Assessment (OTA) estimates that the American surplus in international services trade is grossly understated by official figures. This is discussed in more detail below.

Inadequate Data Base: a Problem for Negotiations

Trade in services means both: (a) the supply of services across borders and (b) their provision by some local presence of a non-national or foreign-owned or controlled enterprise. It is important to keep this distinction in mind when looking at services trade data problems.

In the first type of transaction, services trade has been difficult to define due to conceptual problems in classifying transactions. If a British tourist visits Paris the amount of money he spends there shows up as a service export in the 'travel' category of French invisibles trade data. If the same British tourist flies to New York on a Pan Am flight, his ticket payment to the foreign airline is counted as a British service import in the 'passenger fares' category. If a Japanese company ships goods from Okinawa to the United States and pays for ship-handling services at the American port, this counts as an American service export under 'transportation'.[13] Thus, the export of services by a country can be a mixture of domestic services provided to touring foreigners and other services supplied across borders; few such transactions involve imports or exports in the traditional sense.

In the second case, the need for the simultaneous presence of consumer and supplier — which may be due to the non-storability of services (probably their most salient characteristic) or to the importance of a personal relationship between supplier and client — tends to limit the tradeability of services and contributes to a blurring of the distinction between trade and foreign direct investment. Depending on the definition and status of a local presence, the sale of a service may be classed either as an import or as domestic production via foreign direct investment. To complicate the matter further, many services are provided by multinational enterprises with a number of offices in different geographical locations working together simultaneously. The value added is diffused geographically, but the final fee may be booked at a particular location for tax or regulatory reasons.

The ability to operate abroad and the capacity to increase the tradeability of services are being transformed by technological advances which make it easier and cheaper to utilise data banks and advanced communication services. These advances have been the driving force behind the creation of a wide range of new products and services. The growing quality and efficiency of telecommunications make more services internationally tradeable including international banking and commercial insurance activities and several business-related services. In this respect governments are finding it difficult to keep up with developments in their monitoring of international service transactions. Profitable computer 'export' sales, for instance, may actually appear in trade data as 'imports' which refer to the fee booked by leading banks and multinationals for processing in their home office data transferred electronically from their subsidiaries and customers in other parts of the world.

These and other important statistical issues have been analysed in an important recent study by the U.S. Office of Technology Assessment, a congressional research agency. According to its report on trade in services, the volume of American international trade in non-banking services and the size of the U.S. surplus are far larger than reported in official IMF and U.S. government statistics.[14] Table 8 compares the three sets of figures.

Table 8: Summary of U.S. Trade and Foreign Revenue Figures for Services[a] (at current value of U.S. $ billions)

	TRADE			FOREIGN REVENUES	
	Exports	*Imports*	*Balance*	Overseas revenues of affiliates of U.S. firms	U.S. revenues of affiliates of foreign firms
IMF figures					
1983	39.4	35.9	3.5		
1984	41.4	41.5	−0.1	Not compiled	
U.S. gov. figures					
1983	41.8	35.4	6.4		
1984	43.8	41.5	2.3	Not compiled	
OTA estimates					
1983	67–84	52–66	17[b]	87–97	69–75
1984	69–91	57–74	14[b]	Not available	

a. Excluding banking
b. Based on mid-range of OTA estimates for exports and imports
Source: Office of Technology Assessment, and IMF.

The report estimates that in 1984 the American trade surplus on services was 14 billion dollars, although official government figures place it at only 2 billion dollars while IMF data make it slightly negative. The agency argues that both sets of official figures, which are almost identical, understate direct exports of non-banking services by between 25 and 47 billion dollars and imports by between 16 and 33 billion dollars. The OTA's estimates of the surplus are based on taking the mid-range of the two sets of figures. Similarly, in 1983 the U.S. trade surplus totalled 17 billion instead of the 3.5 billion dollars calculated by the IMF and the 6.4 billion dollars recorded by the U.S. Department of Commerce.

Furthermore, as Table 8 shows, the report emphasises that sales of services in foreign markets by the overseas affiliates of U.S. companies exceed by a considerable margin direct exports of services. Thus, affiliates of American companies abroad had service sales totalling between 87 and 97 billion dollars in 1983. Similarly, service sales in the United States by affiliates of foreign firms were also far larger than direct service imports: according to the OTA, direct imports were between 52 and 66 billion dollars in 1983, while service revenues of foreign affiliates were estimated to be between 69 and 75 billion dollars. The report underlines the necessity of including sales of foreign affiliates, as well as the standard balance-of-payments measure of exports (receipts) and imports (payments), in a comprehensive assessment of international service activity. This reflects more realistically the two basic alternatives for selling services overseas: direct export of services (as in the case of a licensing agreement which can be considered as an export of an intangible asset or right), or an operation via the establishment of a foreign affiliate such as in a joint venture.

The OTA study, like other surveys carried out in recent years, draws attention to the extent to which the IMF and national government figures are flawed by several serious inconsistencies and omissions resulting from inadequate information gathering, problems in assigning value to services, and failure to update statistical methods. The national studies on services trade carried out under GATT auspices all generally agreed that better coordination of data gathering is necessary to provide countries with an expanded data base for more effective analysis.[15] Clearly, the very large uncertainties in the data (as illustrated by the ranges estimated by the OTA), and the lack of analytical expertise on trade and investment in services, make it much more difficult to evaluate the importance of services trade, either taken as a whole or on a sector-by-sector or bilateral basis. This in turn impairs the ability of governments to define negotiating objectives, evaluate possible concessions and develop effective negotiating positions. More statistical work needs to be done to help negotiators understand where the competitive strengths of their major service industries lie in relation to those of other countries, be they in more advanced technology, financial services or other service sectors.

Competitive Dynamics

So far only relatively scant attention has been paid to the dynamics of the service economy and even less to the conditions that shape international competition in service markets. Negotiators who have committed themselves to elaborating rules for individual service sectors will find it difficult to speak with confidence about the factors which determine negotiating issues without a better knowledge, than seems to exist at present, of the economics of service markets. This is a serious problem in two respects: first, substantial differences exist between service sectors in terms of market characteristics and competitive dynamics which will necessitate appropriately differentiated negotiating approaches in devising sectoral rules; and second, the fact that some service sectors are developing very rapidly challenges negotiators to anticipate what direction these developments will take and to devise rules which will be appropriate for their future management. Traditional factor analysis may not be of much help in understanding what comparative advantages one country has over another and to what extent these may shift within and between countries.[16] In order to come to a better understanding of the driving forces which determine the flow of international trade in services, it will be necessary to go beyond the country-specific comparative advantages of traditional theory — natural resource endowment, levels of labour skills and wages, and cost of capital — and incorporate at least two other factors which play a major role: corporate strategies and new service infrastructures.

Corporate Strategies

Corporate strategies not only refer to the important factor of entrepreneurship, but encompass the totality of managerial skills, marketing and production techniques, distribution networks, training methods, new ways to understand and relate to customers, and innovative uses of information. This combination of skills and organisational resources is itself a relatively new and powerful determinant of international service flows, particularly because multinational corporations (MNCs) are dominant in several service sectors.[17] In a multinational competitive setting, the specific mix of factors critical to company performance depends to some extent on the specific situation but some general factors have been recognised as crucial.[18]

1. *Responding efficiently to market needs:* many services — in particular, transportation, distribution, much insurance and accounting — are intimately linked with trade in goods; the value of many goods depends on the availability and the quality of services. Nowhere is this more true than in the case of the freight industry, where freight costs can account for up to 20 percent of the final sales value of a product. With manufacturers continuously looking to increase efficiency in the freight sector, shipping companies have been responding by increasing the range of services offered. The door-to-door aspect, which means not only combining more than one mode of transport to shift goods from manufacturer to retailer, but also the provision of finance, insurance, storage and related services, all of which demand sophisticated management, has become so important that the ship is no longer the central part of the business.
2. *Having a clear identity:* effective strategies start with a clear business definition of a company's product and more generally of its specific identity. The success of Gilbert Trigano's Club Méditerranée (Club Med), Europe's largest tour operator, is based on an effective combination of services for which the guests, known as 'GMs' or *gentils membres*, pay one all-inclusive charge in advance, covering air fare, transfer from airport, meals, a wide range of sporting and cultural activities, and a strong element of direction and identity provided by the 'GOs' or *gentils organisateurs* in each of the Club Med villages. The current challenge for management after three decades of success is to prevent the original concept from becoming stale by incorporating constant innovations — winter ski resorts to protect against seasonality, extra sports, computer and language courses particularly for the Japanese, conference or training packages in exotic locations for corporate customers — all within the basic concept, in order to keep an identity which distinguishes it from its competitors.[19]
3. *Adapting to local conditions:* leading service firms, particularly those engaged in businesses with a high degree of customer contact, may find it desirable or even essential to staff their operations with nationals of the host country. A Club Med village, for instance, normally employs between 200 and 300 local citizens and prefers local purchases to imports even if these are more expensive. In developing countries, in particular, this kind of wealth creation has proven useful by increasing their management's negotiating power in matters such as

work permits for the GOs of various nationalities who organise activities in each village and the provision of infrastructure and other public services.

4. *Control:* a central question in multinational service operations is the degree to which local policies and procedures should reflect local requirements as opposed to those of the company. The basic issue concerns the cost and quality of the service performed. Accounting and advertising services — both culture sensitive — are normally provided by people located in the client's market: copywriters in London, as a rule, will not be capable of carrying out an effective campaign in Italy. As a result, the foreign affiliates of advertising companies operate more or less autonomously in terms of production and billing. International advertising companies are thus usually structured as a conglomeration of largely independent units, the common interlinking factor being the coordination of affiliate services for multinational clients. Generally, the structure of companies which specialise in the international sale of services, such as accounting, law and engineering, tends to be complex and rather loose.

An example of tighter international control and standardisation is McDonald's. The successful international franchising concept of the McDonald's hamburger chain combines rigorous purchasing and operating controls with the entrepreneurial drive of its franchisees.[20] McDonald's management demands high product and service quality in each restaurant and the rigid operating procedures, covering everything from hygiene to the temperature of the fat to fry the potatoes, are designed to assure consistency. In a celebrated legal battle with its franchisee in Paris, the company fought to win back its name claiming that Raymond Dayan, the franchisee and subsequently the founder of the O'Kitch chain, did not meet company cleanliness standards. On the other hand, the company allows its franchisees to develop a local appeal which include a few menu modifications, such as adding beer in Belgium and West Germany or tea in Britain. In effect, McDonald's sells a management system and not only a product.

New Service Infrastructures

In addition to the role of corporate strategies as a source of comparative advantage in the service economy, more needs to be understood about the importance of the new service infrastructure. Just as industry cannot function without the traditional infrastructure of energy, communications and transport systems, the service sector is increasingly dependent on new computer and communications technology. This opens up new trading opportunities in services that can be delivered electronically: video and audio entertainment, computer programming and data processing, publishing, advertising and public relations, and communications and information services. Many multinational companies use communications channels to transmit organisational or managerial services, such as accounting and financial reporting between parent company and subsidiary or between subsidiaries. The greater economies of scale that result from the centralisation of internal management functions have encouraged the sale of such services on the same communications channels to third parties: Citibank, for instance, sells access to financial data and Boeing Computer Services supplies data processing services worldwide.

The value of communications networks emphasises the need to understand better economies of scale which are not commonly assumed to apply to service industries. While some labour-intensive and skilled personal services that directly bring together producer and consumer may resist economies of scale, the structure of other service industries means that significant efficiencies can be reached when the service is provided on a wide, multinational basis: in both passenger and freight transport, the provision of bulk services enhances affordability, and in the retailing trade the strategy of mass merchandising, as the name itself implies, has had a significant impact on costs. Questions about the role of multinational corporations, and their well-known ability to adjust to trade barriers and investment regulations, clearly apply to several service sectors where their dominance is marked. In certain cases it is conceivable that it would be easier for governments to deal directly with multinationals without rules rather than conform to an internationally agreed code. Product cycle and productive capacity may have some relevance but probably less than insights into human and organisational capital, the key elements of what has been discussed as corporate strategy.

Technological change is modifying the face of service industries worldwide making it necessary for governments and businesses to adapt to this change. The technologies for data processing and dissemination are creating a substantial potential for economies of scale, but whether such change is bringing increased competition or greater concentration of control differs from sector to sector. Where competitive forces have been released governments are finding it necessary to adopt at least some measure of deregulation. The effects of deregulatory pressures are particularly important in communication services where concern for national security and personal privacy is encouraging the introduction of restrictions on the international flow of information. The main international implications are that technological change and deregulation cannot be contained within national borders given the emergence of international networks and global access to information sources which are increasing economic interdependence.

Leading International Service Sectors

The extent to which combinations of these factors are creating or limiting the opportunities for free trade depends on how they operate in a particular sector. Here we face the old problem of generalisation versus differentiation among services. It is beyond the scope of this paper to offer conclusive analyses of what is happening in all major service sectors, but several of the factors described above, particularly in terms of the interplay of technology, corporate strategy and government policy, have an important impact on multinational competition in three sectors — transport, financial services and telecommunications — which are undergoing major regulatory reform in certain markets. These three sectors are explored below. In addition, developments in the professional business sector, comprising accounting, advertising and consulting, will be reviewed as an example of a set of international service industries which are generally less hampered by physical, financial or regulatory barriers than most other services.

Transport

In both air and maritime transport, forces moving the industries towards more liberal trade are in conflict with the protectionist policies which governments have traditionally used to regulate their transport industries in order to provide incentives for the development and maintenance of national flag carriers. The following sections will highlight the extent to which a balance is being struck between the protection of national interests and the dynamics of open competition.

Civil aviation: unlike other service industries civil aviation is governed by a coordinated worldwide system of bilateral agreements which regulates air transport. The system is based on the Chicago

Convention of 1944 which clearly stipulates that each state has complete and exclusive sovereignty over airspace above its territory. The shooting down of the KAL 007 flight over the Soviet Union in 1983 was the latest brutal reminder of the inviolability of national sovereignty of airspace.

The global network which links pairs of states in over 1,500 bilateral treaties will not be quickly dismantled. Nearly every country is committed to a national 'flag' airline and seems prepared to meet any cost in terms of subsidies in order to keep it flying. If competition were free on a global basis only a small number of International Air Transport Association (IATA) carriers would remain viable — free competition will, therefore, not happen.

Nevertheless, the process of liberalisation has begun, notably in the United States, the largest market in the world where American internal airlines carry more passengers than the rest of the world put together. It should be remembered, though, that despite American advocacy of free trade in services, the U.S. government has never been, and is still not, prepared to let foreign airlines compete for a slice of its domestic market. Several economists believe that the traditional heavy regulation of the airline sector has allowed serious inefficiencies to develop. Current U.S. experience since deregulation in 1978 is now helping to provide some conclusions about the international applicability of deregulation.

Proponents of more competition argue that the freeing of the industry from government regulation has increased efficiency by lowering fares, forcing airlines to cut costs and to compete for more passengers. In the United States, managers have reduced union power in the face of competition from new, non-unionised airlines, labour costs have been cut back and fare wars have broken out in rapid succession. The most innovative of newcomers in this regard was Donald Burr, founder of People Express, who, according to one observer, 'concentrated everything on cheap fares, reducing costs to a minimum with his skeleton staffs he could undercut every other airline, and his costs in 1984 were 3.25 cents per seat-mile — the lowest, he claimed, in the history of air travel.'[21] Cutting costs is not the only way to become more efficient: airlines have also been trying to fill more seats and reduce the idle time of aircraft. However, since phased deregulation took final effect in 1984, a remarkable consolidation in the U.S. domestic airline business has occurred and the many mergers and acquisitions have removed much local competition, stabilised air fares and strengthened the position of the big seven American operators (Pan Am, TWA,

Delta, Texas, United, American and Northwest Orient) who between them now carry an estimated 80 percent of U.S. domestic air travellers.[22]

In Europe, protective governments are wary of full-scale deregulation but are increasingly under pressure to liberalise the system. Although there are legitimate doubts that adequate safety standards can be maintained under conditions of complete deregulation — evidence for which can be seen in the large fines imposed on major U.S. carriers in 1985 — self-interest on the part of airlines and governments is the key force maintaining the cartel of high fares and market-rigging arrangements in Europe. Both strong airlines, like Air France and Lufthansa, and weak ones, such as Olympic, oppose attempts to diffuse low fares. Initiatives at the level of the European Community are unlikely to get far given the widespread uncertainty among European airlines and governments about which airlines could survive in open market competition. Prospects are better for some less restrictive bilateral agreements on routes, equipment and services between European states. These will not result in a completely free market but will establish a network of more open bilateral deals in which at least a portion of the service between two countries will be opened to all operators. Airline privatisation in Europe, such as the planned flotation of the world's largest international non-U.S. carrier, British Airways, should facilitate the liberalisation of air fares in the longer term, although much attention will first need to be paid to the management of the sale, and in particular to its most valuable intangible asset, its allocation of lucrative routes.

Shipping: rapid changes in technology have revolutionised the provision of services in the maritime transport industry. In particular, the development of intermodal containerised cargoes has allowed the use of more fuel-efficient vessels, has facilitated cargo storage and loading and has helped shipping companies to become masters of both land and sea transport, providing a total service for the shipper.

Shipping companies, such as Sea-Land which pioneered containerisation in the 1950s, have invested heavily in rail, road and shipping equipment to improve their total door-to-door transport networks (known as intermodalism) and thus achieve economies of scale of vertical integration. Shipping is in a fiercely competitive condition and with several lines fighting for survival, the range of services on offer has been increasing. Moreover, the shipping industry has responded to the increase in international trade with hardware and management technologies, which have substantially reduced the unit cost of transport.

The scheduled liner trades (container and other services) have so far escaped the overcapacity and cut-throat competition which has plagued tankers and bulk carriers. However, at present, at least one of the toughest companies in the business, Taiwan's Evergreen Line, is launching round-the-world services that are expected to create havoc. In addition to threatening the liner companies themselves, an outbreak of competition will also threaten the system of regional cartels — called conferences — which govern the container trades by regulating price competition and fixing market shares for national carriers. Conference power seems to be on the wane, and many now predict that the conference structure will not survive the global shipping challenge.

Round-the-world services will make it even more difficult for non-traditional maritime countries to develop a presence in international shipping. Given the large capital investments required and the high level of management sophistication, the access of developing countries to the freight market is limited. Developing countries have been attempting to ensure market shares for existing or emerging national fleets through political action rather than commercial competition. The most notable example in this respect has been the U.N. Code of Conduct for Liner Conferences (1983) whose essential feature is to allow exporters' governments to split cargoes three ways: 40 percent for their own ships, 40 percent for those of the cargo's destination and 20 percent for the free market. As such, it impedes competition in transport rates in an attempt to increase revenues and secure a larger market share for countries that are not members of the OECD. Negotiations on liberalisation will have to take into account fundamental differences regarding national sovereignty and trade philosophy, as many governments attempt to guarantee the profitability of their shipping industries through domestic regulations and international agreements which restrict price competition and fix market shares for their national flag carriers.[23]

Financial Services

It is now widely accepted that capital moves with increasing freedom in financial centres across the world in pursuit of the best available returns, and that these flows are increasingly independent of trade in goods. According to Peter Drucker, 'capital movements unconnected to trade — and indeed largely independent of it — greatly exceed trade finance.' He cites two sets of figures to support this conclusion: first, the London Eurodollar market, where the world's financial institutions borrow from and lend to each other, turns over 75 trillion dollars a year, a volume about twenty-five times the size of world trade; second, foreign exchange transactions, in which one currency is traded against another, run to 35 trillion dollars a year — twelve times the worldwide trade in goods and services.[24]

There seems to be no single explanation for the emergence of capital flows of such magnitude but the speed of change is such that the politics and economics of deregulation in the capital markets have received less attention than they deserve. Deregulation in one financial market inevitably leads to some deregulation in another if the latter wants to remain attractive to investors. Thus, the American decision in 1984 to scrap the withholding tax on interest payments (a key factor in driving U.S. borrowers to the Eurobond market) led West Germany, France and the United Kingdom to follow suit in the same year. Exchange controls have been liberalised in the United Kingdom, Japan and Australia, giving further momentum to deregulation in other countries. Restrictive dealing practices are being relaxed; the British, for example, abolished fixed commissions on international securities dealing in 1984 and are following this up in the domestic market in the so-called 'big bang' of October 1986.[25] Switzerland's stock exchanges are revising their commission structure and the big five Swiss banks are reducing commissions on Swiss franc bond issues.

At the same time, protectionist measures to exclude foreigners from domestic markets have been made counterproductive by developments in technology and the huge increase in financial instruments of all kinds. More efficient markets are being demanded by users as technology is put in place. In time there will be total electronic and twenty-four hour trading around the world. Companies such as Nomura Securities and Merrill Lynch do not depend on the services of domestic stock exchanges if they are judged too expensive or exclusive. Part of the reason for the British initiative to deregulate the Stock Exchange is to stop the drain of international and domestic securities trading to New York due to high transaction costs and a dealing system out of tune with international practice.

Although there are differences in the political motivation for deregulation in different countries, the common characteristic is the drive to stimulate competition and attract more international financial business. In Japan, change is coming faster than many bankers predicted when the Japanese government embarked on its programme of financial liberalisation in 1984. Whatever the motives for liberalisation (some feel that its aims are to help fund the budget deficit and import the necessary banking skills which Japanese institutions must learn in order to be competitive), Japan has been opened to the currents of the world capital and currency markets by the liberation of interest rates and yen trading and by the decision to admit foreign banks to key financial sectors, such as the securities business, the stock exchange and the primary government bond market. Overall, the pronounced deregulatory drive reflects the intense competition between different financial centres (key statistics for which are presented in Table 9) and also the inability or unwillingness of governments and central banks to resist the changes that the accelerating pace of international capital flows is forcing upon them.

As far as the banks are concerned, these changes are apparently quite timely because they coincide with the trend towards investment banking. Commercial banking (the taking in of deposits and their conversion into loans in the traditional way) is now less important than investment banking (the business of raising funds for customers by underwriting and dealing in securities). For many capital users securities finance is cheaper and more flexible than bank loans. With tight government monetary policies limiting the expansion of banks in the foreseeable future, entry into securities has become for many banks the only road to growth. However, the commitment and costs of setting up competitive securities operations in the world's major markets are daunting. Successful banks will need the widest possible geographical reach, an ability to deal in all the big financial markets, a strong dealing team in securities backed by top-class research and technology, and a wide range of institutional and corporate contacts. International banking is going through a fundamental process of change. Traditionally, it was the jealously guarded flagship of each sovereign state but now it is under pressure to become a single and highly competitive world market with a much wider choice to borrowers and investors. Corporate strategy, once a luxury the banks could do without, is now a condition of survival. Nowhere is this better illustrated than in the case of three leading international banks: Citicorp, Barclays and Sumitomo.

Citicorp, the world's largest banking organisation, aims to be all things to all people in the financial services industry. It has one of the most impressive global securities operations with government bond dealerships and stock exchange seats in London, Tokyo and New York. Structurally, Citicorp is adapting to international change

Table 9: Foreign Participation in the Three Leading Financial Marketplaces

	London	New York	Tokyo
Foreign banks	399	254	76
Foreign stock exchange members	22[a]	33	6
Foreign dealers in primary government bond market	12[a]	2	29
Share of international banking market (1985) %	24.9	15	9.1
Share of foreign exchange turnover (1984) %	32.6	23.3	5.3
Stock market turnover £ bn (1985)	52.8	671.3	271.5
Stock market capitalisation £ bn (end 1985)	244.7	1,302.2	648.7

a. incl. UK firms partly or wholly foreign-owned
Source: *Financial Times*

by merging its investment banking and treasury operations, arguing that they belong together as they both deal in capital markets. Nevertheless, in the United States under the Glass-Steagall Act, Citicorp, as a bank, is prevented from underwriting securities for corporate clients.

Barclays of London, the United Kingdom's second largest bank and twelfth in the world, is basing its international strategy on the view that banking and securities operations will continue to converge and, thus, the need to create a leading international securities operation will continue to grow. Barclays is helped by the fact that of the three leading financial market places, London alone allows banks to freely enter investment banking. Barclays recently bought a stockbroker and a jobber which are being merged with its merchant bank to create an investment bank, Barclays de Zoete Wedd, in order to take advantage of opportunities in the investment banking sector.

The world is gradually coming to acknowledge the strength of Japanese banks. Among the largest ten banks in the world listed by assets (shown in Table 10), five are Japanese. In recent years, Japan's biggest financial institutions have increasingly looked for business abroad. Relatively quickly they have become key players in most of the big international banking markets, particularly in lending and foreign exchange. In the United Kingdom, for instance, they do more foreign currency lending than either the British or American banks. Despite the large amount of business they conduct

Table 10: The World's Ten Largest Banks By Assets (as of 31 Dec. 1985)

	Bank	Country	Assets ($ bn)
1.	Citicorp	USA	174.0
2.	Dai-Ichi Kangyo Bank	Japan	158.3
3.	Fuji Bank	Japan	142.7
4.	Sumitomo Bank	Japan	135.9
5.	Mitsubishi	Japan	133.5
6.	Bankamerica Corp.	USA	129.5
7.	Banque Nationale de Paris	France	123.8
8.	Crédit Agricole Mutuel	France	123.6
9.	Sanwa Bank	Japan	123.5
10.	Crédit Lyonnais	France	112.1

Source: *The American Banker*

around the world, the international presence of Japanese banks is geographically quite limited, due to government restrictions on the opening of branches abroad. Sumitomo, for example, Japan's third largest bank and fourth in the world, has only twenty-nine foreign branches compared to Barclays' eighty or Citicorp's ninety-three. Despite the handicap of being prevented from entering more fully into securities trading by Japanese banking law, Sumitomo is determined to move into investment banking wherever it can as part of its overall goal of becoming Japan's first all-round financial conglomerate.

Information Services

The growth of information as a key resource in the international economy is based on the convergence of telecommunications and computer technologies which permit data to be generated, stored, processed and sent anywhere in the world via electronic networks. The world's markets for currencies, commodities, financial instruments and securities depend on real-time electronically transmitted information through the use of worldwide communication networks. The operations of banks, credit card companies, the insurance industry, airlines, shipping industries, travel agents, estate agents and hotel reservation systems, engineering project management houses and on-line data publishing houses are similarly dependent. Technology allows for rapid aural, visual and data communications between any two places in the world, which means that companies can now sell to faraway markets without personal contact. Although there is a lack of statistics on volumes and types of information flow, the LOTIS committee, which lobbies on behalf of British invisible trade earners, reckons that most of the data stored and transmitted across frontiers is internal company information with a growing proportion — probably over 30 percent — being bought and sold.[26]

Financial information in its various forms appears to be the industry's driving force and information systems are already sophisticated enough to supplement, if not yet to replace, physical market floors for trading. One of the best-known examples is the Reuters' foreign exchange dealing system where deals are struck almost instantaneously on screen and a paper record is supplied nearly as quickly. Reuters dominates the market for financial services in the United Kingdom and provides data to over 17,000 subscribers of its business information services, which cover foreign exchange, money markets, bonds and most stock exchanges, and futures and commodities markets in the world.[27]

Banks are among the major users of electronic forms of transfer with their own national, regional or international systems. The common adage 'time means money' is nowhere more apt than in banking. The difficulty that a single bank has in acquiring all necessary information has provided the incentive for banks to join together on a global basis to develop an industry-wide network with limited participation. It was in order to help meet the need for fast and reliable ways of transmitting banking instructions internationally that SWIFT was established in 1973 with 250 shareholding banks in Europe and North America. SWIFT's membership has since grown to 1,400 participants in sixty countries and the society has developed into one of the largest global communication networks, enabling banks to transmit banking messages worldwide virtually instantaneously. Designed at the outset to handle 300,000 messages daily, the system currently processes more than 750,000 with over half of SWIFT's business coming from only fifty banks. While the traditional business of message processing and transmission remains SWIFT's core service (accounting for an estimated 80 percent of the society's total revenues), now faced with competitive pressures from groups such as Reuters and from the PTTs, which have become more dynamic since liberalisation, SWIFT is also expanding its range of services (including the supply of terminal equipment and related software, and the handling of communications for the ECU clearing system).[28]

Information networks are also being used at the public level and public data networks are proliferating at a remarkable rate.

According to some industry estimates there are already several thousand data bases in the United States with revenues totalling around one billion dollars in 1984 and projected to rise to 10 billion dollars by the end of this decade.[29]

Major electronic information providers have been recording substantial increases in the number of subscribers and revenues in recent years. Leading services in the United States with over 100,000 subscribers include H & R Block's broad-based Compuserve Information Service, the financially oriented Dow Jones news/retrieval service and Mead's professionally oriented Lexis/Nexis/Medis service. While the voracious appetite of investment banks for data will be the major source of market growth, providers of information services also base their optimism on the increasing penetration of microcomputers into all aspects of business and professional life. At relatively small cost, an individual located in any country with a modern communications system and an appropriate regulatory policy can connect his personal computer to a telephone line in order to obtain access to information stored in any data base. Data bases are moving out of the offices of librarians and specialist researchers onto the desks of end-users, of middle managers, in particular, who are becoming increasingly adept at directly obtaining and manipulating electronic information. In this, they are being helped by the trend towards producing 'relational data bases' where information can be analysed in several different ways, depending on the individual requirements of the end-user.

Telecommunications play a central role in the international trade of information-based services as they are the main channel of distribution for these services. Telecommunications and information services are subject to a significant amount of government regulation via the control of the main channels for the provision of these services (for example, leased lines and satellites), usually by public telecommunications monopolies (PTTs). The PTTs have traditionally supplied all forms of communication services domestically and internationally and represent formidable bastions of government control. The regulations limit the right of access to data banks and communication networks and limit foreign participation in the market through restrictive licensing policies and high taxes.

France has raised duties on imported computer software, relating the duty not only to the price of a tape or floppy disc but also to the value of the research behind the software. New Canadian banking regulations stipulate that data be processed and kept inside Canada. On the grounds that governments have a legitimate role to play in the protection of the users of telecommunication services, Sweden's data privacy laws prevent its data from being processed in unregulated 'data havens,' existing elsewhere. Some governments use regulations to develop local systems and aid the activities of local producers: Brazil, in particular, has attempted to control information flows in and out of the country since 1979, restricting external data processing and insisting on the use of local computer equipment.

PTTs in many countries, especially those of West Germany, Austria and Belgium, impose high charges in considerable excess of the telecommunications capacity employed for interconnecting with foreign-located data banks and processing facilities. This has the effect, even if not intentional, of encouraging the use of domestic data services and leads to the protection of domestic data-processing jobs.

Thus, many of the trading issues and fears which arise in this field are based on the fact that the communications infrastructure in most countries is controlled by government-owned monopolies, the majority of whom prefer existing arrangements. However, the situation is changing since a number of countries have deregulated in order to provide a greater variety of services at more competitive prices both nationally and internationally. The United States led the way with the deregulation of its telecommunications industry, the break-up of AT&T, and the removal of restrictions allowing the telecom companies to enter data-processing ventures. As a result, the American business communications market has become much more dynamic in terms of equipment and services offered.

Elsewhere, the United Kingdom, Japan and Canada have also initiated varying degrees of liberalisation. In the British case, liberalisation measures have provided a wider choice of more competitively priced equipment and services and British Telecom has responded to the challenge of competition by cutting its long-distance and international rates and launching a number of new services. The psychological impact of British policy on other European countries has been considerable. In West Germany the government recently established a committee to examine whether the Bundespost, the German PTT, is capable of responding to change quickly enough, and in the Netherlands, official proposals to increase competition in the supply of telex, telephone and data services are being debated publicly. Moreover, several large multinationals, concerned about the negative effects of government restrictions on their global communications systems, have been strongly supporting moves to negotiate freer trade in telecommunications services in order to strengthen worldwide access to communications systems at desirable cost levels.

Given the huge worldwide potential for information services, the stream of innovative methods for producing more efficient and lower cost services, and the free trade impetus provided by deregulation and multinational business, national governments and their PTTs are finding it increasingly difficult to resist pressure to lower barriers to competition. If trade negotiations cannot tamper with the sovereign rights of governments to decide their own telecommunications policies, they will at least have to come to grips with the international consequences of national policies when these policies adversely affect other countries' trading interests.

Professional Business Services

The key professional business services — accountancy, management consulting and advertising — have a clearly multinational character, with many of the firms established in scores of countries and their foreign earnings accounting for a substantial part of their revenues. The 'big eight' American accounting firms generate over 40 percent of their total billings from work done outside the United States. The growing internationalisation of these core business service sectors is directly linked to the postwar rise of the multinational corporation. As large domestic manufacturing and service firms widened their international operations, accountants, consultants and advertisers followed suit in order to serve their clients worldwide. These professional services have generally been less hampered in their expansion by regulatory and financial obstacles than have international banking and insurance.

In the accounting industry, the multinational company Coopers & Lybrand was established in 1957 when the British firm Coopers merged with the American company Lybrand. This enabled Coopers to follow Unilever into the American market and enabled Lybrand to serve the growing European business of the Ford Motor Company. McCann-Erikson, which won the Esso advertising account in 1911, grew internationally with the oil giant.

Multinational companies are the biggest spenders on advertising: one recent Saatchi survey showed that eighty-seven of the United States' hundred biggest advertisers are multinationals with over half of them in the process of centralising their advertising operations. Ten years ago, less than 13 percent of world advertising expenditure was handled by international agencies, a figure which has now risen to around 20 percent. As more companies' brands sell globally, and media, such as cable television, become more international the pressure increases on multinationals, such as Beatrice Foods, Kodak, Olivetti, IBM and Colgate Palmolive, to streamline their communications in terms of financial and other resources. With operations in seventy-five countries, Unilever relies for the bulk of its advertising on only four multinational agencies, encouraging them to take a more international view of their client's wants. According to one senior Unilever strategist, 'rather than brief our management in detail in every country on our international advertising needs, we expect our agencies to carry this out for us. If we had one agency in France, another in Italy and so on it would cost a lot of money to keep them all in tune.'[30]

This trend has led to increased activity on the merger front with advertising agencies aiming for the critical mass of worldwide systems and clients in order to provide increased security and stability. The merger in 1986 of three of the world's top twenty agencies — BBDO, Doyle Dane Bernbach and Needham Harper Worldwide — has created what is one of the largest global groupings with annual billings of around 5 billion dollars. The president of BBDO International, Willi Schalk, justifies his company's merger strategy in the following way: 'We believe that in the long run in order to stay competitive you need size, because size guarantees you can win, train, nurture, keep and pay the best talent in the business. And talent is a key factor that provides the quality and creativity on which agencies depend. It's not volume for volume's sake.'[31]

In the challenge to develop global capability and general business skills, the Saatchi group is widely acknowledged as playing a leading catalyst role in the changes underway in international advertising. Begun from scratch in 1970 by the brothers Charles and Maurice Saatchi, the company has grown with a rapidity that few companies in any business can match. It became the biggest advertising agency in Britain in 1979, Europe's largest in 1983 and is now the largest in the world in terms of billings after its 1986 purchase of Ted Bates. Table 11 shows the positions of the ten leading global advertising groups in terms of gross income and billings before the acquisition of the Bates group. Saatchi accounts for over one percent of world advertising business and the aim of the company is not only to lead the world in advertising but in several other business services as well. A series of recent acquisitions — of among others, management consultancy and market research firms, public relations and corporate design companies — have turned it into a business-communications

Table 11: Top Advertising Groups 1985

Rank	Agency	Gross income ($m)	Billings ($bn)
1.	Young and Rubicam	536	3.6
2.	Ogilvy Group	481	3.3
3.	Dentsu	473	3.6
4.	Ted Bates Worldwide	466	3.1
5.	J. Walter Thompson	451	3.0
6.	Saatchi and Saatchi Compton Worldwide	441	3.0
7.	BBDO International	377	2.5
8.	McCann-Erikson Worldwide	345	2.3
9.	D'Arcy Masius Benton and Bowles	319	2.2
10.	Foote, Cone and Belding Communications	284	1.9

Source: *Advertising Age*

Table 12: Leading Management Consulting Firms 1985

Firm	Revenues ($m)	% overseas	Number offices worldwide (total)	Consulting share of total revenues %
A. Andersen[a]	477	26	74	39
McKinsey & Co.	350	50	n.a.	100
Towers, Perrin, Forster & Co.	305	10	n.a.	100
Price Waterhouse[a]	280	50	94	40
Booz-Allen & Hamilton	260	8	n.a.	100
Peat Marwick Mitchell[a]	240	27	88	24
Coopers & Lybrand[a]	201	35	95	26
Ernst & Whinney[a]	188	27	119	23
Arthur Young[a]	175	40	90	30
Hay (Saatchi)	142	55	94	100
Touche Ross[a]	140	40	86	25
Bain	100	10	n.a.	100

a. accounting firms
Source: *Consultants News*, *International Accounting Bulletin*, and author's estimates

group based on the rationale that for many clients such services are inextricably connected. As Saatchi's large multinational clients continue to centralise their own marketing operations, Saatchi's aim is to establish a 'communications superstore' where clients can take what they need off the shelf.

Large accounting firms have long followed a strategy of cross-fertilisation with management consultancy. Consultancy is especially attractive to accountants because growth in auditing and tax, the traditional business of accountancy, has been slowing down whereas consultancy is growing rapidly: in the United States, the world's biggest market, it has revenues of about 4 billion dollars a year. In addition, the Reagan plan to simplify the U.S. tax system threatens to let a big slice of American tax work disappear. As can be seen from Table 12, Arthur Andersen, the biggest accountancy firm in the world is also the biggest consultant with estimated revenues of 477 million dollars, while the traditional and probably best-known consulting firm, McKinsey & Co., is second with 350 million dollars in billings. Other accountancy firms are following the Andersen path: Touche Rosse has made several recent consultancy acquisitions and Ernst & Whinney, another of the big eight accountants, has been rapidly developing its consultancy business.

These big groups are also trying to diversify within consultancy because of the potential for separate divisions to create customers for each other. In one recent case, a leading firm exploited opportunities for synergy when it hired a large number of engineers to carry out a plant study for a client. Although separately contracted, the study won the firm the audit account to replace another accounting firm which the client had long used. This seems to be typical of the trend of serving multinational clients, in many parts of the world, across several lines of business with teams of experts drawn from international accounting partnerships undertaking specialised work. Table 12 gives an indication of the high degree of internationalisation of the top accounting firms in terms of the number of offices they operate worldwide which act as the human and informational resource base for multinational project work.

Internationalisation of Services: Conclusions

This brief review of major service sectors has emphasised the differences between each sector and the factors that shape their competitive profile. The analysis has highlighted the importance of two recent developments: the growth of international trade flows and the significance of multinational corporations which, when considered together, have increased the rate of internationalisation in the service sector. Both developments have been influenced by advances in information technology which have helped to accelerate the tradeability of services and have facilitated the supply of services to foreign markets. These developments have also brought about economies of scale and increased the capability of companies to widen their range of products. Multinational companies — as has been shown above in the areas of finance, information and professional services in particular — are significant suppliers in a variety of service sectors and many of them have been expanding rapidly so as to sell their services globally. The major forces driving this phenomenon of expansion are identified below:

— transborder data flows and the existence of worldwide information networks. Companies with access to such a grid have the potential to offer a variety of services extending beyond those comprising their traditional sector, such as the supply of non-banking services by banks.
— the need of MNCs to expand their operations in order to be able to continue to service their clients, mainly other multinationals. This applies particularly to corporations active in insurance and banking. International insurance operations have traditionally been necessary complements to international trade in raw materials and manufactures. In the banking sector, the presence of multinationals is particularly strong. The multinational banking network has developed rapidly in response to the increasing challenges of international trade and the expansion of the operations of the international financial markets. This phenomenon of expanding international business support services also extends to advertising companies and professional services such as accounting, legal and consulting services.
— the increasing capacity of a relatively small number of MNCs to offer a wide range of services in the world market. Mergers have often been a convenient vehicle and have resulted in the creation of transnational service conglomerates which have acquired the ability to supply several markets with a number of services, or a combination of goods and services. Such mergers have helped to get better access to finance, to maximise the potential of information systems, and to integrate sales of turnkey projects with engineering and other services. In advertising, a small number of

companies dominate the industry and are extending their activities beyond advertising, per se, into market research, public relations and management consulting.

It appears that in rapidly growing, increasingly internationalised service sectors, the size and scale of a country's firms are significant elements of its competitive position in the world market. In some sectors, such as accounting and advertising, the health of a service industry can depend largely on the foreign revenues of the leading companies. These phenomena add a new dimension to international trade in services for which legal systems and national policy makers are not yet prepared. One of the implications is that the established MNCs are in a position to increase greatly their scale of operations and their competitiveness around the world with the result that their subsidiaries in other countries — especially in developing countries — will keep a large degree of advantage over local competitors attempting to offer the same services. This goes some way to explain the fear and intransigence of a number of developing countries in the matter of liberalising trade in services.

III

Trade Liberalisation: Policy Issues and Perspectives

After years of preparatory work the decision taken by GATT ministers, at Punta del Este in September 1986, to negotiate on the removal of service barriers opens up a whole range of practical problems which negotiators are going to have to solve. One of the most important is the need to understand better the nature and importance of existing services trade barriers. Another concerns various aspects of the coming negotiations: the acceptability of the rationale for liberalising services trade; the aims and strategies of the major protagonists; the significance of a north-south divide in the debate about extending the competence of the GATT to cover the new trade area; and (perhaps most important in practical terms) the question of how to proceed in negotiating the liberalisation of services trade. In most of these issue areas the United States has been the *demandeur*, pressing ahead to bring the whole complex of services trade matters to international public attention. In recent GATT discussions, no issue has generated so much interest and dissent as the (at least originally) American contention that the benefits of services trade liberalisation will enhance development and economic growth for both developed and developing countries.

Why Liberalise?

The main aim of the U.S. initiative is to achieve freer trade in services which, like freer trade in goods, Americans argue, will be of benefit to all and will increase total world welfare. The reason to act now rather than later is not only justified by the long list of trade barriers and restrictions that already exist, but also by the probability that technological advance will open up new services trade opportunities which could be better utilised under fair trade conditions, if action were rapid enough to forestall the entrenchment of national interests.

The major stumbling block for U.S.-led demands for a GATT negotiation on free trade in services is, in effect, political. The problem is to convince a sufficient majority of nations that there will be few losers and many winners if markets are opened up on the GATT basis, that a concession to one trading partner in the GATT is a concession to all. It has proven difficult to persuade developing countries, suspicious of the reach of Western multinationals, that they stand to gain from liberalisation. Less developed countries' (LDCs) representatives argue that MNCs and the countries with the most advanced service infrastructure stand to benefit most from a lowering of trade barriers and their dominance in international service markets will increase. Related to this is the concern of many developing countries that they could be the victims of decisions taken by MNCs which are effectively beyond international control. However, opinions differ greatly on these issues. Some LDCs would undoubtedly suffer a temporary balance-of-payments loss. Others, such as South Korea and India, who are substantial exporters of construction and engineering services, may be in a position to gain. It may well be that in many service functions that depend primarily on skilled labour, many developing countries with relatively low labour costs can increase their service exports more quickly than is commonly assumed. In the absence of adequate information, however, it is difficult to appraise the long-term effects of freer services trade policy on single countries.

The standard argument for the opening of markets is based on Ricardo's well-known theory of comparative advantage where the growth of trade leads to the kind of international specialisation in which each agent performs the tasks at which he is most effective. Deregulation has in this sense acted as a spur: the liberalisation of financial services has created many specialisations with large institutions attempting to cover the spectrum and smaller ones finding that there is room for new specialities. However, economic theory is still underdeveloped with regard to services and the literature has not yet fully addressed the question as to whether, and to what extent, the principle of comparative advantage applies to international trade in services.

Since the GATT was set up in 1947, the strengthening of free trade in goods has without doubt promoted economic development. Free traders base their case for negotiating services in the GATT on the fact that trade in services is worth a conservatively estimated 350 to 400 billion dollars per year or about a fifth of all trade. Greater exchange of services could provide a dynamic effect on world economic growth similar to that given in the first three decades of the GATT's existence by successive rounds of tariff cuts on manufactures. The alternative would be discriminatory rules on a regional or bilateral basis which, given the growing importance of services trade and the fact that many services are inseparable from trade in manufactures, could well bring about an irreparable weakening of the GATT system.

The widely diverging views on the rationale for liberalisation — between the developed countries which are determined to establish rules for services trade and the many developing countries that feel they have little to gain from such rules — clearly create a conflict which will not be easily resolved. If services trade negotiations are to lead to a global set of rules, governments and negotiators on both sides will have to find economic reasons for liberalising services trade that will benefit both industrialised and developing countries.

United States: Providing the Initiative

The most noticeable change that has occurred in trading relationships within the GATT has been the transformation from domination by a single country, the United States, to the sharing of power and influence between the United States, the European Community and Japan. The economic dominance of the United States lessened as postwar allies and former enemies closed the gap, benefiting from fewer defence obligations and a more organised government-led industrial development strategy.

Nevertheless, the United States has remained the traditional initiator of trade liberalising conferences and all major rounds have corresponded to a series of renewals of the American Trade Agreements Act, the most significant being the Trade Expansion Act of 1962 (for the Kennedy Round), the Trade Act of 1974 (for the Tokyo Round) and the Trade and Tariff Act of 1984 for the current round.

In 1978, American trade laws were changed to broaden the definition of trade to include both goods and services. Since then, both the Carter and Reagan administrations have been vigorous in their pursuit to inscribe services prominently on the world trading agenda. These efforts have been facilitated by the creation of a specialised services trade staff in the Office of the Special Trade Representative which has been productive in identifying issues and establishing negotiating priorities and approaches.

Services trade is of great importance to the American balance of payments: in 1984, while the United States had a 114 billion dollar deficit in merchandise trade, it had a 14 billion dollar surplus in services. This fact, coupled with the recognition of the rapid expansion and importance of the services sector in the United States — of the 20 million new jobs created in the 1970s, 17 million were in services and manufacturing now accounts for under 20 percent of all jobs — has changed traditional views about trade policy. It is now widely appreciated among more forward-looking politicians, commentators and businessmen that soon freer trade in services will be vital to the American economy.

Moreover, the deregulation of many domestic service industries has added irrevocable momentum to the commitment to liberalise services trade by directly tying in the interests of the manufacturing sector. The freeing of trade in services is of great potential benefit to American producers of goods because service companies, whether communications companies or financial institutions, are prominent among the heaviest buyers of high-technology equipment. The fact that the United States deregulated some services more quickly and more thoroughly than other countries posed a new risk for advanced equipment manufacturers. They now have to compete with foreign competitors in the American market without having comparable access to government-regulated service suppliers in other countries. Clearly, one way to redress the imbalance is to force the pace of liberalisation on an international scale.

The growing interdependence of national service markets have given many service companies an international perspective that was absent only a few years ago. Partly because of technological advances, there is also now a new mix in the kinds of services supplied internationally. This has generated greater interest and caused more concern about barriers to trade in services. The concern has been channelled by lobbying bodies working within the governmental trade policy system, representing an impressive degree of business influence on trade policy formulation. At the policy level, there are two private sector advisory committees — the Services Policy Advisory Committee (SPAC) and the joint Trade Representative-Commerce Department Industry Sector Advisory Committee (ISAC) -- with which the U.S. trade representative must by law consult. Outside the policy process is the Coalition of Service

Industries which serves as the lobby of the major American service sectors.

The extent to which the coming negotiations on services can fulfil the demands of the American service lobbies remains to be seen but will probably play an important role in maintaining congressional support for the new round. The Administration requires authority from Congress to continue the talks and it is likely, given the magnitude of the trade deficit and the eroding domestic support for multilateralism, that there will be greater demands for more protectionist elements.

After years of intensive American efforts to make services a top negotiating priority and to lay the groundwork for the new round, it was no surprise to discern the undisguised joy of the Administration after the GATT ministerial meeting in Uruguay in September. The U.S. delegation came back with everything it wanted including the pledge of the GATT negotiating parties to bring services within the scope of the GATT. According to the Deputy Trade Representative Michael Samuels, the United States has two overriding objectives: 'First, to reach agreement, through negotiation, on a legal framework of rules and procedures that would make trade in services as open as possible; second, to achieve, through negotiation, commitments of a sectoral or functional character dealing with problems unique to individual service industries.'[32] This dual approach has been largely adopted by the negotiating partners as the basis for proceeding.

European Community: a Services Superpower

The European Community (EC) has abandoned its initial doubts about the U.S. initiative and has become a firm supporter of negotiating an international services agreement. However, moving to this position by overcoming policy divisions among member states on services trade questions (and also, significantly, on agriculture) required a drawn-out process of consultation and compromise. In this sense, the long gestation period of services as an international trading issue — from the Brock initiative at the previous GATT ministerial meeting in November 1982 to the compromise of Punta del Este nearly four years later — was in part, due to the nature of the Community's policy formulation process as well as, more significantly, to differences between the United States and certain developing countries.

Table 13: Overview of Market Shares in Services by Region 1984 (in percent)

	Transport	Travel	Other
EC (incl. intra-EC trade)	39	43	48
USA	14	12	9
Japan	11	1	5
Other countries[a]	36	44	38
Total	100	100	100
Total Value in bn $[b]	122	95	143

a. For transport: of which Norway and Sweden represent 6%, Egypt 3%, S. Korea and Singapore 4%, travel: of which Austria and Switzerland represent 8%, Canada 3%, Mexico 3%, other: of which Austria, Switzerland, Norway and Sweden represent 7%, Saudi Arabia 3%, S. Korea and Singapore 4%, Canada 2%, Mexico 2%
b. calculated in terms of invisible receipts
Source: IMF, *Balance of Payments Yearbook*

In conjunction with the national studies that were carried out in the early 1980s and submitted to the GATT, many EC countries discovered in sounding out their trade ministries and service producers that they were among the world's most competitive service exporters. Information technology, advertising and consulting are leading Community services which are expected to grow as a result of liberalisation in international trade in services. Increased competition in such areas, it is felt, will also improve the quality of services available to a range of manufacturing industries.

The Community survey showed that the Community was a service 'superpower' with exports (including intra-Community trade) about three times higher than those of the United States, with France exporting even more than the traditional leader, the United Kingdom. Table 13 shows that in terms of world market shares, measured in invisible receipts as calculated by the IMF, the Community is by far the dominant bloc, accounting for nearly half of total global receipts in the important 'other services' category which includes the most dynamic service sectors. Dominance is also marked in the 'travel' or tourism category. Tourism accounts for about 4 percent of GDP in the Community. In Britain, an estimated 2 million people (almost one in twenty of the workforce) make at least part of their living from tourism, a sector that has been producing 50,000 new jobs a year.

Nevertheless, not all doubts have been dissipated. Most European governments continue to control access to their telecommunications markets for political reasons, such as securing inward investment and job creation. For foreign competitors, such as American computer-service companies which have followed their corporate clients to Europe, PTT regulations in Europe are seen to inhibit the growth of an open market for advanced services. Restrictions may be used to maximise PTT revenues or for more overtly protectionist purposes. In West Germany, for instance, the government has undertaken to introduce new telecommunications rules which are expected to turn over all sales of user equipment to the private sector, but the Bundespost continues to be a vigorous opponent of telecommunications liberalisation, arguing that it is obliged to protect its clients who demand higher standards than elsewhere.

In May 1986, EC External Relations Commissioner Willy de Clerq announced that the Community countries had 'become firm proponents of an agreement on services' and he called upon private sector producers of services to set up an umbrella organisation to seek consensus on what positions should be taken in the new round of trade talks.[33] His statement implies that the services to be treated in the new round will be defined rather broadly to include the supply of services by foreign representations. For example, in the case of banking, which the Commission wants to see included among the trade topics, the European view is that an agreement to liberalise trade in services should cover the establishment and operations of foreign banking concerns, given that most banking services can only be sold abroad by establishing a local branch, subsidiary or agency.

Community interest in services trade rules also has an important internal dimension. The European Community has been engaged since its inception in a slow and tortuous process of removing barriers to trade in services and obstacles to the right of establishment between the member countries. In its White Paper on the completion of the internal market for goods and services, the EC Commission has set a target date of 1992 for the realisation of the common market. In some service sectors this target is proving difficult to achieve. In the area of transport, for instance, very little progress towards genuine liberalisation has been registered in the near thirty-year existence of the Community, mainly due to the problem of reconciling entrenched national interests which defend national road hauliers, airlines and railways. Negotiations on a common market for goods and services, although consisting of a large number of small and detailed questions, touch upon sensitive domestic issues. The United Kingdom, for instance, has been pushing hard for free trade in the insurance business but becomes very defensive when German companies want to make a major acquisition of a British insurance company.

In the end, negotiations on freeing trade in services between members of the Community will depend on the kind of Community — a more closely integrated Europe which can only be made a reality by creating one large market, or merely a looser customs union — that members want to have in the next decade.

Japan: Tomorrow's World Competitor?

Japan has risen to a position of economic preeminence because it has based its economic policies on trends in the world economy on the premise that domestic policies succeed only if they support the country's international competitive position. If anything, this strategy has been almost too successful if one judges by the international tensions over Japan's chronic surpluses.

In keeping with its traditional approach to international trade negotiations, Japan has gone further than any other industrialised country in supporting the American initiative in the GATT. At one level, the Japanese want to be seen as good international citizens and hope that their cooperative attitude on services and on a new trade round will deflect foreign criticism concerning their bilateral trade surpluses with the United States and the European Community. If multilateral negotiations take six or more years, Japan may be able to buy some breathing space.

This will be partly facilitated in the next few years by a process of privatisation and deregulation. In the first case, Japan's small public service sector will become smaller as the Japanese government sells part of its shares in Nippon Telegraph and Telephone (NTT), Japan national railways and Japan Airlines. The main idea in breaking up NTT's monopoly in 1985 was that telephones and computers were converging and that competing private sector firms could best provide new services in a sector playing a central role in the economy. Deregulation and internationalisation is evident in banking and securities: among the measures announced by the government in 1983 was the gradual removal of the barriers between ordinary banks, trust banks, securities companies and other financial institutions.[34]

Over the years, Japan has run a large deficit on trade in services, primarily due to payments for transport and travel, and, except for shipping, it has traditionally had less of a stake in service exports than the United States or the European Community. But this is changing. The Japanese intend to become a significant exporter of services and consequently a strong trading regime will help Japan in the long term.

Several years ago, the Japanese began to target the service sector as a promising growth area and have systematically concentrated financial and manpower resources in the development of services. Rapidly growing sectors, with well-established domestic companies that are exporting at a growing rate, include finance and insurance, construction, real estate, consulting and design, fashion, films and publishing, leisure industries and tourism. Technological breakthroughs, the unique information networks of Japan's large general trading companies, the continuing growth of Japanese manufacturing firms which require the inputs of their affiliates in the service sector, and government policies to standardise communication networks are all playing a role in assisting the worldwide expansion of Japanese services.

Developing Countries: Many Still to be Convinced

The compromise at Punta del Este on service talks resolved the protracted struggle between the United States and several developing countries, led by Brazil and India. The problem lay in reconciling American insistence on having trade in services as a subject in the new round (known in the jargon as a 'single-track' solution) with the developing countries' argument that talks on services should be separate from those on goods ('twin-track'), as the GATT is not competent to handle services.[35]

Many countries have sought to avoid a situation in which they could be forced to trade off concessions on services simply in order to retain their current access to Western markets for goods. In the compromise solution, based on an EC proposal, the ministers, as GATT signatories, declared the opening of a new round to handle trade in goods, and, as sovereign governments, they announced the start of parallel talks on services, technically outside the GATT but under the same overall negotiating committee as goods. Both sides could claim key interests had been satisfied: the United States could state that services were part of the new round, this being the major condition for its participation, while Brazil, India, Argentina, Egypt and other hardline countries felt that they had won what they had fought for, namely keeping the negotiating process on services separate from that on goods.

In spite of the compromise which technically allows the talks to go ahead, the United States will need stronger support from Japan and the European Community to counter the criticisms and fears of some developing countries which remain suspicious of efforts to liberalise services trade. There is a widespread perception among developing countries that what the big OECD countries are really seeking, under the free trade banner, is much more liberal rules on direct investment which would threaten infant industries and limit the sovereignty and autonomy of smaller countries to determine the crucial role of services in their infrastructures. These objections of principle are likely to remain influential as many developing countries firmly believe that benefits from comparative advantage in services will accrue almost entirely to the industrial countries. Indeed, it is difficult to dismiss the argument that in many developing countries sophisticated service sectors such as banking, data processing and telecommunications are too weak to withstand American or Japanese competition.

In this respect, it is worth noting that India's argument that an international system of rules for trade in services should respect national policies is reflected in the wording of the ministerial declaration. However, the fears of developing countries may be misplaced. These countries need to acquire infrastructure and technological services because these play such a central role in the development process. Excessive restriction will mean having to forego opportunities for the transfer of much needed technology and expertise.

Not all developing countries take a similarly negative view of services trade negotiations. There is a wide range of opinion on the objectives of the negotiations, ranging from the oppositional countries in the so-called 'G1O' grouping, such as Brazil, India, Argentina, Yugoslavia and Egypt, to new service centres such as Hong Kong and Singapore which desire an international agreement. The newly industrialising countries, which account for an increasing part of world merchandise trade, are acquiring comparative advantage in certain services as they accumulate organisational and technological know-how, partly through the import of modern services. This trend is apparent in the successful development of the provision of professional services (the Philippines), printing (India) and data processing (Singapore). Singapore is an interesting case in point: this nation is in the top fifteen service exporters and has the highest value of service exports, some 31 percent as related to total exports. As part of a more concerted shift towards services, Singapore is investing heavily in its health care services which, in the form of medical treatment for foreigners, is an important foreign exchange earner. In the construction sector, during the recent period when the Middle East was the main source of engineering contracts, South Korea and several other developing countries were among the world's leading exporters of construction services.

Even the opponents have seen the necessity of joining the negotiations to help ensure that the talks extend to services of immediate interest to their countries or to those in which they may in time gain comparative advantage. However, at this stage, reference to future interests may not be an adequate inducement for many developing countries to participate in multilateral services trade talks. The industrialised countries may have to offer concessions on merchandise trade to allow the negotiations to proceed.

Looking ahead, freer trade in services will probably open up markets initially in the rich OECD countries — whether it be Japan's financial system to foreign investment banks or West Germany's insurance market to British companies — and is unlikely to have much effect on the societies of developing countries for several years. Whatever the exact pace of liberalisation, negotiators will have to come to terms with the many sensitive issues involved in reducing restrictions to services trade and to the equal treatment of foreign and domestic suppliers, restrictions which have their roots in government policies and practices. Some of the most important government justifications for trade and investment restrictions are outlined below.

Government Policies and Trade in Services

Governments around the world have played an important role in restricting the growth of multinational services, justifying such actions in several ways. Many service sectors have been considered critical to the well-being of a country's own economic development, thus justifying *domestic control over key industries*. These sectors are seen to contribute to the maintenance of national independence and their importance is sometimes reinforced by strategic arguments, as in the case of a national merchant navy.

However, the most frequently used arguments refer to the banking system; the prevalent view being that the influence of foreign banks on monetary policy must be limited. It is highly unlikely that the financial authorities of any major country in the world would permit one of their largest banks to be acquired by foreign interests. Britain's Monopolies and Mergers Commission supported the view of the Bank of England in 1981, when it rejected the bid by the Hongkong and Shanghai Bank for the Royal Bank of Scotland, Britain's fifth largest bank. The United States is ambivalent about foreign-owned banks. On the one hand, the country is relatively open with an estimated 20 percent of all American business loans being made by foreign-owned banking institutions. On the other hand, the United States is worried about its openness: in 1980 it imposed a temporary moratorium on all foreign takeovers of American banks and many argue in favour of a new moratorium until a more coherent national, and probably more protectionist, policy is in place.

Governments have also been heavily involved in the development of their country's domestic insurance industries to promote the formation of capital and to ensure a high degree of compatibility between credit and investment policies. West Germany forbids any insurance (except marine) to be placed overseas, and in France insurance cannot be imported. In Belgium, only non-marine business with a premium of less than 1.5 million dollars can be placed abroad. Indeed, the number of countries which restrict freedom to purchase insurance abroad has grown rapidly in recent years. According to Lloyds' of London, ninety-nine countries now try to protect their domestic insurers in this way. Such entrenched government policies against free trade may, in fact, be restricting business for their insurance companies rather than securing it. Under present conditions, multinational companies are prevented from buying cover for all their European risks from one insurance company. Many multinationals, in particular large American companies, have decided to establish an in-house insurance capability to cover many of the risks that would normally have been handled by insurance companies, which are thus left with a smaller share of the insurance market.

Significant trade imbalances have led some countries to restrict services performed by foreign firms and to develop their own industries. This need for *infant industry support* is often quoted by developing countries. By restricting the right of establishment of foreign banks and insurance companies, or by limiting the scope of their business operations, governments attempt to give local firms enough breathing space to allow them to gain experience and efficiency while national infrastructures are built up. Similar policies are also pursued for the country's shipping line, airline, advertising industry and sectors concerned with computer technology and telecommunications.

Brazil's vehement opposition to the inclusion of services in the new GATT round stems from the conviction that freer trade in services would devastate its own infant industries. Although some of its larger companies, such as Mendez Junior in construction and Petrobras in oil technology, can and do compete internationally, the Brazilian government believes the impact of liberalisation on sectors such as banking, insurance and information technology would be decidedly negative. The strength of Brazilian convictions regarding services is rooted in its own postwar industrial development and commercial strategy. Key elements in this protectionist trade policy are 'the law of national similars' which prohibits imports of any products and services where equivalents are available in Brazil. The controversial informatics law, aimed at excluding foreign competitors and, thus, also the latest in micro-electronics in the information technology field, may have damaged efforts to modernise industry but, as supporters of the strategy claim, the law has seen Brazil's computer sector grow from sales of 20 million dollars ten years ago to around 2 billion dollars today.

There are, of course, other motivations for the introduction and maintenance of services trade barriers. *Balance-of-payments support* can play a role in cases of acute shortages of foreign exchange where, for instance, domestic subsidiaries of foreign banks are required to keep increased foreign exchange deposits, or where restrictions are introduced on the transfer of profits from branches established in the host country to the foreign parent companies.

The *consumer protection* argument is used in some countries to prohibit foreign banks from undertaking certain types of business (given the impossibility of gaining access to the assets of the overseas parent bank in case of difficulties). It is also used to justify the existence of more stringent capital and reserve requirements for affiliates of foreign banks and insurance companies. Measures against aggressive and exaggerated advertising on the part of foreign suppliers can also serve to protect domestic consumers.

Social and cultural motives can also be important in imposing trade barriers where some developing countries prohibit the import of foreign films and advertising in order to preserve their cultural identity. Protectionism in this area can take many forms including establishing a minimum percentage of domestically produced television programmes, and taxes on cinema admissions to subsidise domestic film making.

In addition, various kinds of performance requirements have been imposed in several countries aimed at expanding local *employment* opportunities related to particular services. In their efforts to ensure that their countries have an adequate share of the growing services sector, governments may refuse entry, or deny the right of establishment, to foreign firms and independent professions. In the case of public building and construction work, they may restrict the invitation of tenders to domestic firms or grant preferential treatment to domestic suppliers. One of the most controversial cases in recent times was the bidding process for the 4 billion dollars Kansai airport construction project in Osaka, Japan, in which several foreign construction firms claimed that the airport authority effectively excluded foreign bids in favour of domestic companies.[36]

This brief review of motivations shows that not all measures which foreign suppliers have perceived as trade barriers are the result of an intentionally protectionist stance. The coming multilateral negotiations will have to take account of the reasons which underlie the measures acting as trade impediments in order to reach agreement about what can and what cannot be realistically considered as protectionist.

IV

A Possible Work Programme for Services Trade Negotiations

Now that the decision has been taken for the negotiations to proceed, questions arise about what they should accomplish and how they should be organised. According to the ministerial declaration of September 1986, the contracting parties to the GATT agreed on the following:

> Negotiations in this area shall aim to establish a multilateral framework of principles and rules for trade in services, including elaboration of possible disciplines for individual sectors, with a view to expansion of such trade under conditions of transparency and progressive liberalisation and as a means of promoting economic growth of all trading partners and the development of developing countries. Such framework shall respect the policy objectives of national laws and regulations applying to services and shall take into account the work of relevant international organisations.[37]

The overriding objectives of establishing a multilateral framework of services trade rules are thus threefold: first, to expand trade under conditions of transparency and progressive liberalisation; second, to promote economic growth of all countries; and third, to promote the development of developing countries.

In organisational terms, the statement of intention about the direction of the negotiations may imply a process in which the establishing of general and sector-specific rules is accompanied (although not explicitly stated) by an agreement on common and practicable definitions of services trade barriers. How this will work out has still to be determined as there are no agreed principles to serve as a frame of reference. A fundamental problem arises here because many services, unlike goods, cannot be shipped from one country to another but only delivered on the spot. Thus, GATT rules on market access for services will have to cover the right of establishment in the customer's country and, hence, touch upon the issue of a country's autonomy to make its own foreign investment rules.

The following section, which is based on numerous analyses by the OECD, the European Community and the U.S. government, describes a possible negotiating approach along these lines. The key elements of a possible negotiating framework are summarised in Table 14. It is stressed that the order in which the three negotiating elements are discussed below is not meant to imply a strictly sequential process. According to Ambassador Jaramillo, Chairman of the Negotiating Group on Services, deciding on 'the order of business is important: priorities differ, and at least some parts of the work may need to be conducted in parallel.'[38]

Defining Trade Barriers

The kind of preparatory work, which is necessary in negotiations of this sort, has already been undertaken to some extent in the OECD and the GATT. The systematic gathering of facts on barriers to services trade is everywhere still in its early stages. The United States and the OECD have been the driving forces behind the documentation and categorisation of existing barriers and their relevance for international negotiations. In the most comprehensive report to date, more than one thousand trade obstacles were listed by the Office of the U.S. Trade Representative. However, examinations of the problem to date, whether at the national or international organisation level, have been mostly concerned with drawing up enumerative lists which neither highlight the frequency of individual measures nor provide an economic evaluation of the effects of particular barriers on the volume of services trade.

Insofar as the very numerous impediments to trade are susceptible to systematic description at all, one method would be to categorise a few basic types of barriers which are encountered in numerous service industries. Table 15 is an illustrative list of restrictions on cross-border trade, foreign sales of services and the activities of foreign branch offices. The key problems in services include restrictions on the right of establishment, and once established, limits on foreign equity, stipulations on employee nationality, burdensome licensing and certification requirements, limitations on the range of services that can be supplied, national

Table 14: Possible Negotiating Framework for Services

Key Negotiating Elements			
Defining Trade Barriers	Establishing General Rules	Negotiating Sectoral Agreements	Possible Results
— Drawing up of extensive inventory of service trade barriers — Agreement on what is 'legitimate' and 'protectionist'	— Transparency — National treatment — Non-discrimination — Dispute settlement — Market access — Intellectual property — Government monopolies — Separate negotiating group on international information flows (?)	— Sectoral negotiations parallel with general rule talks or commencing after a general agreement	— New codes — General agreement on services with possibility of limited membership — Regional or bilateral agreement

Source: EC Commission, OECD, US Special Trade Representative

Table 15: Illustrative List of Service Impediments

		Transport Air	Transport Mar.	Tele-comm.	Data proc.	Bank-ing	Insur-ance	Cons/Eng.	Advert.	Film ind.	Acc-ount.	Legal serv.	Soft-ware	Hotels motels	Car. rent.
Trade Restrictions	Quant/qual. restrictions	X					X		X	X	X				
	Subsidies	X		X	X			X		X					
	Government procurement	X	X		X		X	X							
	Technical standards	X						X							
	Import licensing		X	X	X		X		X	X					
	Customs valuation			X	X								X		
	Currency controls/transfer restrictions			X		X	X	X		X					X
	Special employment conditions						X	X			X	X		X	
Investment Restrictions	Establishment restrictions					X	X				X				
	Selective taxation					X	X	X		X				X	
	Limits on equity participation			X	X	X	X		X					X	

reservations with regard to government procurement and exchange controls. Definitions will have to be drafted as to what kinds of protection are crucial to national sovereignty as a basis for establishing which barriers can be considered legitimate and which protectionist.

According to the Commission of the European Community, obstacles which take the form of blatantly discriminatory national regulations giving advantage to domestic industry at the expense of foreign competitors would be defined as protectionist; it will be necessary for all participants to accept that such regulations should be phased out in the process of exchange of concessions. On the other hand, not all barriers to services trade are intentionally discriminatory or protectionist. Some service sectors, notably banking and insurance, as discussed earlier, are subject to heavy governmental regulation either due to their significance for national economic stability or in order to protect small savers against the risk of collapse of a company.

Trading partners will have to agree on the scope of what constitutes a legitimate regulation in order to exclude it from the negotiating agenda. However, between the designations 'protectionist' and 'legitimate' there is bound to be a considerable grey area where national regulations will be viewed by some trading partners as objectionable and trade-distorting and by others as justifiable and non-discriminatory. An example of the kind of problem this ambiguity will pose for negotiators is given by Willy de Clerq, the European Community's chief trade negotiator: 'A rule to the effect that branches of foreign banks must employ a host-country national as a manager would be discriminatory, but what about a stipulation that the manager should simply speak the language of the country concerned, so as to be able to communicate with central bank officials, for instance? To some that would appear a reasonable provision, but the Americans consider it discriminatory. Clearly, we can expect protracted negotiations on this sort of question!'[39]

Complicating all discussion of reducing protectionism in banking are two very different ways of looking at the concept of reciprocity. For many U.S. legislators, it means that foreign countries grant American banks the rights and freedoms that foreign banks enjoy in the United States. The opposing view is that the most a U.S. bank can expect when it enters another country are the same rights and liberties given to domestic banks and no more.

Finally, the links between foreign investment and debt will require attention. For many developing countries, particularly those in Latin America with seriously inadequate financial markets, the principal problem is debt. More attention will have to be paid, than has been the case so far, to the linkages between debt, trade and development issues within the context of debtor governments shifting from bank to equity flows as a source of capital. The limitations on rights of foreign establishment will make service negotiations more complex and it remains to be seen to what extent the issue of trade-related investment, which is a subject on the GATT agenda but not within the services framework, will be discussed explicitly by the trading partners. The U.S. Treasury is seeking to exploit the subject in an attempt to remove the national legal barriers which hinder heavily indebted countries from taking advantage of the opportunity to change loans into equity investment by lenders. Although this is in line with the Baker debt-relief programme, in practice companies have been hesitant to take on equity commitments while national regulations hamper them from generating and repatriating profits.

Establishing General Rules

In 1982, the United States started to promote a conceptual framework for trade in services which, after several refinements, essentially consists of first negotiating an umbrella agreement of fundamental principles and rules applicable to services which also allow for certain exceptions. Only after this is achieved would the process of negotiating mutual concessions begin, although a major unresolved issue is whether concessions should be restricted to services or whether trade-offs between goods and services should be allowed. These proposals are now reflected in the 1986 ministerial declaration which affirms the intention of all negotiating partners to establish a multilateral framework.

Essentially, the negotiation of an umbrella agreement would set out a code of conduct that governments would follow in formulating their services trade policies. In contrast to the codes negotiated during the Tokyo Round, which interpret existing GATT provisions, a potential services code would have to go further to include newly defined and binding obligations lacking at present. In addition, the issue of transborder data flows poses a rather special set of negotiating challenges. Work within the OECD forum and elsewhere, in recent years, has proceeded to identify basic concepts which could be applied to the liberalisation of services trade.[40]

In addition to established principles and rules, negotiators will have to confront, in some form, a number of new issues which are raised by the particular character of trade in services. These are discussed in the following review which does not pretend to be exhaustive.

1. Established Principles and Rules

Transparency: the concept of transparency of government policies is a well-recognised trade principle. As argued above, the justification for the definitional phase is to make existing trade barriers and also draft regulations transparent and subject to notification. Until governments and service companies can reach mutually agreed definitions of what constitutes an obstacle, any negotiating effort to halt their proliferation or reduce their impact will be almost impossible.

National treatment of foreign suppliers: they receive the same treatment as domestic suppliers with exceptions in industries agreed to be crucial to the national interest.

Non-discrimination (or most-favoured-nation treatment): this assures foreign suppliers that they will be treated as favourably as those from the country with the most privileged position. However, the question whether non-discrimination can or should be extended to services is likely to prove contentious.

Least restrictive regulations: each government should commit itself to ensuring that regulations are adopted in the least restrictive manner possible.

Due process: in essence, enough time and opportunity would be provided for comment on proposals and for the appeal of administrative decisions.

Dispute settlement: in addition to the established principles there should be an international mechanism for ensuring compliance and for the settlement of disputes by means of an appeal procedure, as provided in the various articles of the GATT.

2. New Principles and Issues

Market access: several service industries want the negotiations to define access to encompass the establishment of a company under local law where cross-border trade is not possible. This area covers the right to set up operations in a foreign country, to sell services in conditions of fair competition, to use a brand name, to have access to the distribution system for public and private markets, and to acquire qualified personnel. Although several countries see this as an investment rather than a trade issue and argue that it should, therefore, not be treated in the talks, the United States and the European Community will be pressing for acceptance of the view that where domestic regulations necessitate a local presence in order to do business, then the right of establishment should be a negotiable trade issue.

Intellectual property: closely related to trade in services will be the attempt in the Uruguay Round to negotiate rules to curb the abuse of patents, copyrights and trademarks. Cheap imitations of many quality goods are costing world trade up to an estimated 100 billion dollars and are causing certain services, such as software, to be plundered. Despite the work of the World Intellectual Property Organisation, the weaknesses of existing international agreements on intellectual property have become increasingly apparent. Foreign counterfeiting and piracy are seriously damaging markets for innovative companies including those for computer software, publishing, advertising, music and communication. The music industry, for instance, is worried about the development of the digital audio tape which can reproduce at very low cost the high quality of a compact disc recording. To quote another example, in distribution, an area in which trade is expanding, franchising has not become established in West Germany because of the lack of any legislation guaranteeing the repatriation of royalties. Key problems are that the international spread of the counterfeiting industry is difficult to combat and that current intellectual property agreements have not kept up with technological advances which leave new and significant intellectual properties without protection. Negotiations within the GATT could bring a number of advantages including the application of GATT mechanisms for the settling of disputes.

Government monopolies: a framework of rules for trade in services will have to take account of the fact that there are profound differences of view between countries about the appropriate role of government in various service industries, about competition between government-owned monopolies and private firms, and even about the desirability of government regulation affecting the standards of services supplied to citizens and to business and finance. In order to promote competition there has been a major effort in several countries to privatise government-owned or government-controlled service operations, but in most countries many domestic services will continue to be provided by public enterprises. The key negotiating issue will be to devise rules to promote fairer competition between private firms and government monopolies (and also in some cases deregulated monopolies) which subsidise both loss-making service operations at home and bids for business abroad.

In the sensitive area of service-delivery systems, especially computer-telecommunications systems, a government monopoly can use its dominant position in various ways to limit competition. The German Bundespost, for instance, is highly restrictive in deciding what equipment may be connected to the Bundespost lines and their charges for lines are determined politically with little reference to market demands. Analysis so far has tended to emphasise the monopoly powers and defensive attitudes of national PTTs, but also seems to indicate that most governments recognise that information technologies and international information flows are crucial for future economic vitality: they want change but not disruption.

3. *International Information Flows*

The GATT declaration of September 1986 does not directly address the issue of freer flows of telecommunications and information services which are becoming more important to international trade. It will not be easy to handle the complex issues involved in the on-going GATT process and negotiators may well decide to deal with the liberalisation of information flows in a separate and perhaps parallel working party. The overall priority should focus on the reduction of barriers which have numerous and often overlapping causes: a whole web of regulatory restrictions emanate from the monopoly powers of PTTs to control technical standards, network access, pricing and supply of equipment; and distortions arise from government regulations which control data privacy and copyright and from government subsidies, bureaucratic bottlenecks and a variety of taxation and exchange control measures.

The existing regulatory environment may, in fact, be causing less disruption than are fears about potential new regulations which could further restrict trade in services and increase costs for companies in terms of operations (tariffs) and administration (compliance with local data-processing requirements). As the LOTIS Committee has recognised, the challenge for negotiators will be to develop policy measures to control information flows for legitimate economic and social reasons, while keeping to a minimum their trade distorting effects. In this sense barriers that cannot be eliminated should at least be made transparent, but this well-recognised principle will be difficult to implement in the information field due to the large number of policies — telecommunications, trade, fiscal, cultural and legal — which affect the international flow of information. A notification procedure will be necessary but the definition of the protectionist content required to trigger the procedure will be problematic.

Sectoral Negotiations

The September declaration of what the negotiating parties intend to achieve includes the 'elaboration of possible disciplines for individual sectors' but begs the question of how this should be organised and how many separate service sectors should be treated. The situation is complicated by the significant differences in the degree to which particular service sectors are subject to protection. According to one analyst, the largest potential pay-offs will probably be found in sectors which have a marked trade potential, a relatively high level of initial protection and limited political constraints on negotiability.[41] Particularly in the case of international information flows, the rapidly changing technological environment and its effect on the delivery of services may well require that talks covering technology, information networks and regulatory policies parallel the general rule-making talks.

Bigger problems will arise when it comes to moving from reciprocity (balancing concession against concession), as at present, to equal national treatment (allowing foreign competitors to do what domestic competitors can do). Even the smallest liberalisation measure usually necessitates a matching concession from the partner concerned. Nomura Securities, the world's largest securities house, only received its banking licence from the Bank of England when the British National Westminster Bank finally gained access to deal in securities on the Tokyo Stock Exchange.

Looking at what came out of the Punta del Este meeting, it seems reasonable to suppose that the trading partners may decide to develop an umbrella agreement of overriding principles which applies to all services (with some exceptions) and which would provide the basis for sectoral liberalisation and for increased trade in services. In this respect, Aronson outlines a possible scenario in which work first begins on an umbrella agreement. After the rough outline of an agreement is reached, sectoral negotiations would begin either in separate groups or within a single negotiation. Work on reducing barriers to trade in specific sectors would be carried out as the concrete details of a general agreement were being negotiated.[42]

Existing Arrangements

The new negotiations on services will have to take into account a number of existing international arrangements to regulate services trade.[43] The GATT itself covers services trade to a small but growing extent; during the Tokyo Round services were dealt with at the margins. Among the codes that were negotiated the government procurement code covers services linked to the delivery of goods.

An important forum dealing with services trade is the OECD. Earlier efforts at liberalisation among member countries (embodied in the codes of Liberalisation of Capital Movements and of Current Invisible Operations) constitute considerable experience in the area of services. More recent work aims at identifying how basic trade concepts, many of which have been discussed above, can be applied to the liberalisation of trade in services. The OECD remains an important focus of interest and has committees handling shipping, telecommunications, insurance, tourism and the financial sector.

International agreements have traditionally regulated shipping, civil aviation and communications and UNCTAD, in particular, has been active in maritime transport, although its liner conference rules tend to restrict rather than to free trade. The existing international regulatory framework of the International Telecommunications Union (ITU) provides the infrastructure for international telecommunications. In the World Intellectual Property Organisation (WIPO) activity has been underway to reach agreements on knowledge-based services such as software, trademarks, copyrights and intellectual property.

Possible Results

An optimistic four-year limit has been set for the completion of the Uruguay talks. Earlier GATT rounds have regularly exceeded their schedules and this one is the most ambitious and complex yet. Tackling the issues within services alone will be complicated enough but relating these to the long list of negotiating subjects under the so-called Track 1 (trade in goods) to achieve an overall balance of concessions will be formidable.

A simple listing of the eleven negotiating subjects already indicates the dimension of the problem: Track 1 comprises talks on tariffs, tropical products, natural resource-based products, textiles and clothing, agriculture, GATT articles, safeguards, subsidies and countervailing measures, dispute settlement, and the 'new' issues of intellectual property rights and trade-related investment which, as we have seen, are directly relevant to the services negotiations. Significantly, governments are committed to tackling for the first time the issue of all direct and indirect subsidies in agriculture. On safeguards, negotiations will aim to establish a new and strengthened surveillance capacity which is to be buttressed — and this again is a unique negotiating development — by a range of rule-making measures to reinforce the role of the GATT.

It is too early to judge the chances of success in these areas, but one crucial problem facing negotiators will be how to settle the individual issues, more numerous and more complex than in the Tokyo Round, and how to weave them into a package which will be acceptable to the main, if not all, trading countries.

What kind of an agreement could negotiations be expected to produce? There seem to be two serious possibilities:

— First, existing and/or new codes on the model of those negotiated in the Tokyo Round could be developed which would apply to all ninety-two contracting parties, or, perhaps more likely, they would only apply to those countries acceding to them. The standards code negotiated in the Tokyo Round which applies to all agricultural and industrial products could usefully be extended to cover such services as telecommunications, where performance and other standards prevent foreign firms from competing with domestic networks. Decisions will have to be made about whether a new code would apply to services generally (which should permit flexibility in dealing with the different characteristics of various service industries) or whether codes should be agreed upon for individual services or groups of services. This latter possibility could well be used to reach agreements that address the specific problems of individual service industries.

— Second, a general agreement on services trade could emerge from the trade negotiations which would regulate both trade and investment in services. The trading partners aim to reach agreement on a legal framework of rules and procedures that would expand services trade and make it more open and transparent. In theory, such a general agreement would consist of basic GATT concepts as well as new rules governing investments which would reflect the importance of service sector income generated by foreign investment and the fact that major international service industries are highly regulated.[44] Such an agreement is quite possible, given the commitment of the negotiating parties to the establishment of an overall services framework. As there are no tariff equivalents and, thus, no measurable concessions in services trade, one problem negotiators will face is reaching accord on the nature of obligations of services trade rules. A framework agreement would open a new chapter in the forty-year history of the GATT. It is conceivable that such an agreement could be administered through the GATT or, alternatively, could have its own secretariat.

How many countries are likely to be covered by new trading rules? Unanimous GATT commitment to a services agreement is desirable but given the well-known hostility of many developing countries to the trade in services issue, it is possible that many will refuse to join negotiations that could lead to a general agreement. In that case, the OECD countries, which account for over 75 percent of global services trade, and perhaps the ASEAN states, may concentrate on establishing a more liberal services trade regime among themselves in some sort of GATT-plus grouping. However, this will by no means be a straightforward task.

Governments of the developed countries have not yet established a common approach on services trade issues nor have they agreed on common priorities. The European Community, which has the potential to provide an example of a functioning common market for services, has had limited practical success in coordinating policies on liberalising services. In any regional solution, the benefits from liberalisation would accrue in the first instance to the participants in the agreement. Another possibility, that of bilateral services trade agreements to facilitate special reciprocal arrangements for particular markets, while possibly proving to be more efficient for the countries concerned, runs the danger of further fragmenting an already weak multilateral trading system.

Conclusion

Efforts to liberalise international services trade in the years ahead will face a number of significant problems which are rooted both in the turbulence of the international trading environment and in the unique character of services trade.

Experience from previous trade rounds has shown that the major elements of a successful trade agreement are shaped by prevailing conditions and attitudes. In the Uruguay Round, the diffusion of international economic power, the recent uneven development of the world economy, growing pressures towards protectionism and defensive government attitudes about the costs of structural adjustment have played the major part in dictating the negotiating issues and will be decisive in shaping the timing and outcome of the agreements. In this sense, there will be only limited scope for negotiators to affect the overall course of the negotiations.

The postwar economic order has been based on rules and institutions designed to reduce barriers to commerce by multilateral agreements assuring similar treatment for all nations. The rapid growth in world trade following the founding of the GATT contributed significantly to world economic growth and welfare. However, responses to the economic strains and to some extent the stagnant trade performance of the late 1970s and early 1980s have raised serious questions about the capacity of the liberal trade principle to solve the major trade issues likely to be encountered in the coming years. GATT rules do not now apply to a large portion of trade and according to some estimates well over half of world trade is subject to quotas, orderly marketing arrangements and a variety of non-tariff barriers. Textiles and agriculture are effectively outside GATT coverage as are much high-technology trade, trade-related investment issues, intellectual property questions and, of course, traded services.

The new round of international negotiations will not succeed unless progress can be made in bringing a much larger part of world trade under GATT principles. There has been a serious erosion of confidence in the GATT system, one that should be halted and reversed if international trade is to increase and support a more general recovery. Reinforcing the GATT through new rules on international trade in services would amount to a significant step forward. However, progress on services trade talks may be held hostage by the problem of reconciling the protectionist demands of troubled industries with the need for increased economic efficiency and trade liberalisation. A considerable degree of political support will be necessary on the part of several major powers in order to move towards liberalisation in such sectors as agricultural products, steel, textiles and pharmaceuticals where trade growth potential, but also trade friction, are greatest.

Negotiators will also have to confront a unique, and as yet not clearly defined, set of problems relating to services trade itself. The approaches to liberalising trade in services are still largely fragmentary, even after the considerable preparatory work done in the years leading up to the GATT ministerial meeting of September 1986 which launched the latest round of trade talks. The preparatory studies do not provide much guidance on the crucial questions of which services should be considered, whether GATT rules should be extended to trade in services or whether a separate self-contained agreement should be worked out, and how to reach broad agreement on the content and coverage of the talks at the start of negotiation among national service industries and governments. More attention will have to be given to how technological advances are affecting the evolution of the international service economy in order to avoid the negotiations concentrating on issues of past and present concern but not necessarily of future relevance.

Trade in goods and trade in services are different and the rules designed to govern them cannot be identical. Negotiators will have to make a serious effort to develop a conceptual framework that acknowledges the particular characteristics of services trade, and takes into account the rapid technological advances in data processing and telecommunications which are opening up opportunities for considerable expansion of international service transactions. Governments have not been able to keep up with many of these advances and have responded by introducing haphazard regulatory measures which differ from country to country. Only a few countries have so far begun to analyse the trading interests of their banks, their insurance companies and their information technology industries and to draw up coherent negotiating policies. At present there is no well-defined concept of services nor are there adequate statistics. There is still a need to know more about the facts; efforts underway to improve the measurement of international services trade must be continued. It is also necessary to develop an inventory of the various trade barriers and trade-distorting measures in order to arrive at a smaller list of generic issues that can be addressed by international rules.

Protectionism in the area of services means restrictions on foreign investment as much as barriers to trade. Negotiations will certainly be made more complex by the need to address the problem of limitations on rights of foreign establishment and ownership. As governments are playing a growing role in both the areas of international information flows and foreign investment rules, an effective negotiating framework which aims at balancing international rights and obligations will inevitably result in some kind of limitation on government sovereignty. Services in all countries are subject to differing degrees of government control and regulation and, as such, touch upon sensitive issues of national sovereignty and the legitimate role of government.

The developing countries, which are generally net importers of services, are greatly concerned about the role of informatics and telematics in infrastructural development and their potential loss of sovereignty in these areas. Although the fears of developing countries may be misplaced — it is precisely in the area of infrastructure and technological services that imported inputs can be most essential in the development process — it will be difficult to convince these governments that trade liberalisation is not a zero-sum game: there are gains for countries that expand their exports but also for those that increase their imports. It is likely, therefore, that the developing countries' present suspicions of services trade liberalisation will require the industrialised countries to reduce significantly their levels of protection for those agricultural and manufactured products of greatest interest to the developing countries.

A greater effort must be made by service companies and governments to educate society at large about what is happening and what needs to be done. This means improving our understanding of the service economy in general and of the particular issues involved in traded services. A prerequisite for successful negotiation to remove national barriers is that service companies understand the subject matter better and present a coherent strategy to trade negotiators. This applies to efforts to mobilise private companies and government officials in order to encourage trade liberalisation not only in the developing world but also in the industrialised countries. Illustrative of this was the recent call by the European Community's trade commissioner to the European service industries to play a significant role in the debate by establishing an EC-wide coordinating body representing the Community's service companies. Without private sector support negotiations could stray off course or run the risk of becoming completely irrelevant.

In the end, however, the progress of international negotiations will depend on the presence or absence of real political commitment to a successful outcome on the part of the major participating governments. This means not only a commitment to begin the negotiations but also a commitment to a timetable to bring the talks to a conclusion sooner rather than later. Domestic and international political consensus is the prerequisite for the successful negotiation of international commitments. The experience of the Tokyo Round of negotiations indicates that much work is still needed to bring about such a consensus by the end of the decade. The industrialised countries will have to take a common stance and although broad agreement has been reached between the United States, Japan and the Community on the desirability of services trade negotiations, the process of reaching substantial agreement is still in its very early stages.

The negotiating parties are in the process of deciding whether to pursue initially an across-the-board approach which, compared to the sectoral approach, allows for the balancing of interests either among sectors in individual countries or among countries. The Americans are confident that negotiations on an understanding to produce basic ground rules could begin immediately and be concluded relatively quickly, but this optimism does not seem to be widespread. Decisions on which specific sectors should then be addressed and their priority order will be part of the negotiating process. On this point there are indications that entry into concrete discussions may only be partial and not global in nature. Progress is most likely to be made within the nucleus of the OECD countries, perhaps on a reciprocal basis. Visible advantages with regard to liberalisation would then provide a strong motivation for individual developing countries to participate. Such an outcome, however, would not add to the effectiveness of the multilateral system. This will only be strengthened by more forward-looking trade policies and by a greater degree of international economic cooperation than currently exists.

Notes

1. On the question of defining services there is no consensus of opinion in the literature. For detailed discussions see Ronald K. Shelp, *Beyond Industrialisation: Ascendancy of the Global Economy* (New York: Praeger, 1981); and J. Gershuny and I. Miles, *The New Service Economy* (London: Frances Pinter, 1983).
2. See, in particular, Netherlands Economic Institute, *The Service Sector and Technological Developments* (Rotterdam, April 1985).
3. U.S. Dept. of Commerce, *1986 U.S. Industrial Outlook*, (Washington, DC). This weighty 648-page annual survey analyses the prospects for over 350 U.S. industries.
4. Japanese National Study on Trade in Services submitted to the GATT in October 1984.
5. 'Japan Survey,' *The Economist* (7 December 1985): 25.
6. See Ian Hargreaves, 'Service sector key to job growth,' *Financial Times*, 26 April 1983. He argues that in the search for more employment, advanced economies, such as Britain's, will depend increasingly on service sector growth.
7. See 'Can Jack Welch reinvent GE?' *Business Week* (30 June 1986): 40 ff. In its strategic emphasis on technology and services, GE has in recent years sold 190 subsidiaries worth about 6 billion dollars and has acquired 70 new companies to the value of 11 billion dollars. Key acquisitions in the service sector have been the financial services group Employers Reinsurance (1984) and investment bankers Kidder Peabody (1986).
8. James Heskett, *Managing in the Service Economy* (Cambridge, MA: Harvard Business School Press, 1986), 103. This excellent study contains a wealth of material on how a wide range of service companies operate.
9. The Stock Exchange Automated Quotations System (SEAQ) became operational in October 1986 as the electronic market place of the London Stock Market. Although the trading floor will continue to be used, there is in theory no need for brokers/dealers and so-called

market-makers to visit the Stock Exchange building.

10. Heskett, *Managing in the Service Economy*, 161.
11. 'International Banking Survey,' *The Economist*, (22 March 1986): 15.
12. In the search for a new theoretical framework for comprehending long-term social changes in the industrialised countries, several models have been proposed including Daniel Bell's 'post-industrial society,' Alvin Toffler's 'third wave' and Dennis Gabor's 'mature society.' In Japan, an important organising concept is Yuichiro Nagatomi's 'softnomics' which focuses on the increasing importance of information-oriented and knowledge-intensive activity and their implications for society and the economy. In Europe, the EC research programme on forecasting and assessment in the field of science and technology (FAST programme) has included work on the challenges facing Europe caused by the internationalisation of services.
13. Shipping transactions in particular are subject to statistical discrepancies. The bulk of the discrepancy is due to the under-reporting of shipping credits. This is partly to do with the phenomenon that the cargo of a ship sailing from A to B may change hands several times when at sea, generating margins for each trader every time a deal is made, margins that are virtually untraceable.
14. See Office of Technology Assessment, *Trade in Services — Exports and Foreign Revenues*, Special Report, U.S. Congress, (Washington, DC: OTA, September 1986). At the global level, GATT negotiators are well aware that service trade data are in urgent need of improvement. According to Ambassador F. Jaramillo, Chairman of the GATT Group of Negotiations on Services, 'one should not neglect the need for more precise data on services. Liberalization in services cannot be foreseen without adequate data on service flows, which is not the case today.' Address to the Symposium on the Liberalization of International Trade in Services, International Chamber of Commerce, Paris, 9 December 1986.
15. See GATT, *Services: Analytical Summary of Information Exchanged Among Contracting Parties*. Internal note by GATT secretariat, (Geneva, November 1985), 26–9.
16. The most widely known theory of trade, developed by Heckscher, Ohlin and Samuelson, builds on the work of Ricardo. It explains comparative cost advantages in terms of the relative abundance of the inputs of labour, capital and raw materials. In the more recent work done on the economics of services, various authors have attempted to identify the factors which are more significant in determining comparative advantage in trade in services than in goods. Several have stressed the importance of human capital and organisational know-how in this regard. In particular, see Jagdish N. Bhagwati, 'Splintering and Disembodiment of Services and Developing Nations,' *The World Economy* (June 1984); Leif Edvinsson, *Trade in Thoughtware and Internationalisation of Services*, unpublished paper (Stockholm, 1986); and for a treatment of R&D inputs, Raymond Krommenacker, *World-Traded Services: The Challenge for the Eighties* (Dedham, MA: Artech House, 1984).
17. See the study by Henri Schwamm and Patrizio Merciai, *Les*

Entreprises Multinationales et les Services (Geneva: Institut de Recherche et d'Information sur les Multinationales, 1985).

18. Corporate service strategies are dealt with by Albert Bressand in a conference paper presented at Ditchley Park, February 1986, 'Services, Corporate Strategies and GATT Negotiations.' A detailed documentation on multinational corporations in the service sector is provided by F. Clairemonte and J. Cavanagh, 'Transnational Corporations and Services: The Final Frontier,' *Trade and Development: An UNCTAD Review*, no. 5 (1984).
19. 'Club Med: the bourgeois holiday camp,' *The Economist* (12 July 1986): 80–1.
20. An overview of McDonald's global operations is given in 'McWorld?' *Business Week* (13 October 1986): 60–5. The conventional McDonald's franchise involves an investment of about 350,000 dollars to cover equipment, signs, seating, decor, working capital and various deposits. Franchise fees of around 12 percent are paid to the company. Generally, the franchisee gets the lion's share of the profits (or losses) and is free up to a point to run the business as he wants. In return the franchisee has to purchase his supplies from the franchisor. Franchising grew up in the United States and fast food still accounts for the bulk of the business but the idea is spreading to other service industries such as cleaning, printing, health care and even funeral parlours. The United States is the world's biggest exporter of franchises, and in 1983, 400 American groups had around 24,000 franchised outlets around the world.
21. Anthony Sampson, *Empires of the Sky* (London: Coronet Books, 1984), 173. People Express, trapped by its own policy like Laker, was for some time on the verge of a merger, take-over or bankruptcy. It has recently been acquired by Texas Air.
22. See 'Europe's Air Cartel,' *The Economist* (11 November 1986): 19–23.
23. A very useful study of the issues in international shipping is provided by Elliot Schrier *et al.*, *Outlook for the Liberalisation of Maritime Transport*, Thames Essay, no. 44 (London: Trade Policy Research Centre, 1985).
24. Peter Drucker, 'The Changed World Economy,' *Foreign Affairs*, 64, no. 4 (Spring 1986): 782.
25. So far nobody seems to have claimed credit for coining the phrase 'big bang.' It refers to the structural changes which have reformed the London Stock Exchange. They came into effect in October 1986 in order for London to capture a leading role in the expanding global securities market.
26. British Invisible Exports Council, *International Information Flows: a Report by the Liberalisation of Trade in Services Committee (LOTIS)* (London, February 1986). LOTIS was formed in 1982 to evaluate the international climate for service trade negotiations and to coordinate the United Kingdom private sector response to issues in liberalisation.
27. Peter Smith, '24 hours, 7 days a week: Financial services around the globe.' Paper presented to the European Services Symposium, Brussels, May 1986. Peter Smith is International Communications

Manager, Reuters Holdings plc.

28. For an up-to-date assessment of the development of the SWIFT network see 'Information Technology in Finance,' *Financial Times* supplement, 16 October 1986, 9.
29. 'Electronic Financial Services,' *Financial Times* supplement, 24 March 1986, 6.
30. Statement by Ken Fraser, Unilever's head of marketing, quoted by Feona McEwan, in 'Agencies catch the merger bug,' *Financial Times*, 7 May 1986. Mergers are also characteristic of the current state of accounting. The rationale for the recent merger of Peat Marwick Mitchell and Klynveld Main Goerdeler (KMG) to form the world's largest accountancy grouping was based on the perception that the needs of the companies' clients were becoming much more international which demanded faster and better balanced development of worldwide coverage.
31. *Financial Times*, 7 May 1986.
32. Remarks of Ambassador Michael Samuels to the European Service Symposium, Brussels, May 1986.
33. Willy de Clerq, 'The European Community and GATT Negotiations in Trade in Services,' speech to the Lugano Economic and Financial Symposium, 27 May 1986.
34. See Kazuo Nukazawa, *Implications of Japan's Emerging Service Economy*, Keidanren paper, no. 8, (Tokyo, 1980).
35. 'GATT — Launching the New Round,' *Financial Times*, 22 September 1986, 6; and 'Les Etats-Unis ont atteint leurs objectifs dans le domaine de l'agriculture et des services,' *Le Monde*, 22 September 1986. The United States originally hoped that the GATT ministerial meeting in November 1982 would launch a new trade round in which services would be a key element. Although the Americans were forced to scale back their ambitions at that juncture they continued to build support for discussing trade in services. An important step was taken at the GATT meeting of the contracting parties in November 1985 when several industrialised countries with the support of certain developing countries argued for the inclusion of services in the new round. At the close of that meeting, a preparatory committee was set up to develop a plan for the new trade talks. The declaration of the 1986 Tokyo summit called for the early launch of a new GATT round and stated that it should address trade in services among the 'new' issues.
36. See 'Banzaï sur l'aéroport du Kansaï,' *Libération*, 23 October 1986, 10.
37. Quoted from Part II of the Ministerial Declaration on the Uruguay Round, GATT Press Release (Geneva, 25 September 1986), 11. On the organisation of the negotiations, the declaration states:

    > Gatt procedures and practices shall apply to these negotiations. A Group on Negotiations on Services is established to deal with these matters. Participation in the negotiations under this Part of the Declaration will be open to the same countries as under Part I. GATT secretariat support will be provided, with technical support from other organisations as decided by the Group on Negotiations on Services.

The Group on Negotiations on Services shall report to the Trade Negotiations committee.

Regarding implementation of the results under Parts I and II, the declaration specifies;

When the results of the Multilateral Trade Negotiations in all areas have been established, Ministers meeting also on the occasion of a Special Session of CONTRACTING PARTIES shall decide regarding the international implementation of the respective results.

According to Ambassador F. Jaramillo, Chairman of the Group of Negotiations on Services, this means that 'all options regarding the legal status and the institutional framework of an agreement on services remain open until the decision is taken.' Remarks made to the Symposium on the Liberalization of International Trade in Services, International Chamber of Commerce, Paris, 9 December 1986.

38. Remarks to the ICC Symposium (see note 37).
39. Speech by Willy de Clerq (see note 33).
40. The Trade Committee of the OECD has carried out substantial analytical work on various goals and principles for free trade, not all of which have been reviewed in this section of the paper. See in addition Jonathan D. Aronson, *Trade in Services: An Agenda for International Trade Negotiations*, unpublished paper, University of South California, February 1986, which sets out some thoughtful proposals on the modalities and objectives of service trade negotiations. A developing country's view is offered by Deepak Nayyar in 'International Trade in Services: implications for developing countries.' Exim Bank of India Commencement Day Annual Lecture, Bombay 1986. He argues that it is not feasible nor desirable for developing countries to establish a multilateral framework across-the-board for all services.
41. See Peter H. Gray, 'A Negotiating Strategy for Trade in Services,' *Journal of World Trade Law* (September/October 1983).
42. See Aronson, *Trade in Services: An Agenda for International Trade Negotiations*, 42 ff.
43. One organisation which is reviewing the extent to which existing rules, standards and agreements can be used to develop a new service trade framework is the Atwater Institute is Montreal which aims to 'preserve and enhance international trade and exchange in information and information-intensive services and manufacture.' For example, the Institute has drawn attention to the possibilities of using the Chicago Convention of 1944 as a model for a global policy framework in the field of information flows.
44. Krommenacker, *World-Traded Services: The Challenge for the Eighties*, 167–79.

Recent Atlantic Papers

Special Issue	Germany in an Era of Transition by Martin J. Hillenbrand
N° 54/55	Public Images of Western Security by Gregory Flynn *et al.*
N° 56	Europe versus America: Foreign Policy in the 1980s by Baard Bredrup Knudsen
N°57	The Changing World Information Industry by Satoshi Kuwahara
N° 58	The Impact of Technological Change in the Industrial Democracies: Public Attitudes Toward Information Technology edited by Richard D. Vine
N° 59/60	The USSR in East Asia. The Changing Soviet Position and Implications for the West by Georges Tan Eng Bok
N° 61	Western Economic Policy Toward Eastern Europe by Heinrich Vogel
N° 62	The SDI and European Security Interests by Louis Deschamps

N° 63 Western Europe: Technology and the Future
by Stanley Woods

At least four Atlantic Papers are published each year. They may be ordered singly or on a subscription basis. For details of subscription rates and orders for Atlantic Papers prior to No. 62 write to:

The Atlantic Institute for International Affairs
9 Avenue Hoche, 75008 Paris, France

Tel: 42.25.58.17

Atlantic Paper No. 62 and all subsequent papers should be ordered from: (all orders must be accompanied by payment)

Croom Helm Ltd
Provident House, Burrell Row, Beckenham, Kent BR3 1AT, England

Orders and Enquiries: Tel: 650 6061